GALE GAND'S
BRUNCH!

GALE GAND'S
BRUNCH!

100 FANTASTIC RECIPES FOR THE WEEKEND'S BEST MEAL

GALE GAND
WITH CHRISTIE MATHESON

PHOTOGRAPHS BY BEN FINK

CLARKSON POTTER/PUBLISHERS
NEW YORK

Published in the United States by Clarkson Potter/
Publishers, an imprint of the Crown Publishing Group, a
division of Random House, Inc., New York.
www.crownpublishing.com
www.clarksonpotter.com

CLARKSON POTTER is a trademark and POTTER with
colophon is a registered trademark of Random House, Inc.

Library of Congress Cataloging-in-Publication Data
Gand, Gale.
   Gale Gand's brunch! / Gale Gand—1st ed.
      p.   cm.
   Includes index.
   1. Brunches.   I. Title.
   TX733.G35   2009
   641.5′32—dc22   2008036988

ISBN 978-0-307-40698-9

Printed in China

Design by Laura Palese

10 9 8 7 6 5 4 3 2 1

First Edition

It's not easy living with a pastry chef. You laugh, but it's true. So I'd like to dedicate this book to my sweet, loving husband, Jimmy, for putting up with the hard parts of having dozens of cupcakes and soufflés and scones being baked and shoved at him for testing practically every day. You don't get any pity from others, love, but you get it from me. You are a gift I'm not sure I deserve, but I sure do appreciate you.

I would also like to dedicate this book to my children, Gio, Ella, and Ruby, for giving me a family to cook for and for filling my life with endless joy, really.

CONTENTS

INTRODUCTION 9

DRINKS 15

BRUNCH BASICS 39

MORE EGGS 59

PANCAKES, WAFFLES,
FRENCH TOAST & OTHER SWEETS 79

THE BAKERY 105

BRUNCH BITES 125

MORE SAVORIES & SOME SIDES 145

SALADS & SOUPS 163

FRUITS & CONDIMENTS 181

MENUS 200

EQUIPMENT & INGREDIENTS 202

ACKNOWLEDGMENTS 205

INDEX 206

INTRODUCTION

"Come on over for brunch!"

That's my favorite invitation to give—and to receive.
I'm obsessed with brunch. I adore making it and I
adore eating it. The food is delicious, and I love the
way it often straddles the line between sweet and
savory. Plus, brunch can be so much easier and more
relaxed than dinner. And if I'm going to entertain at
home, it needs to be easy and relaxed!

I have three kids, and as my family has grown (and my friends' families have grown), preparing and hosting a dinner party has become a complicated endeavor. A weekend brunch party is much simpler to pull off. People can bring their kids, so they don't have to worry about finding a sitter, and your own kids (and theirs!) can help you prepare the meal.

And people seem to have time to stop by for a two-hour brunch—a heaping spoonful of ham and asparagus strata or a slice of Quick Pear Streusel Coffee Cake, maybe—on a weekend morning, even if they don't have three or four hours free at night for dinner. Brunch lends itself to feeling casual and laid-back, though it can still definitely be a celebration. Just pour your guests a Champagne Pimm's Cup and see how festive the morning becomes!

Because I think brunch is such a wonderful way to entertain, I have wanted to write a brunch cookbook for years. Recipes for brunch food can be accessible to all levels of home cooks, and there's usually a role for the kid-chefs in the household too. And even if I'm not entertaining and I'm just making brunch with my family, I love taking the time to sit down together to eat and then send the people I love off into their busy lives with a good, inspiring first meal of the day.

Another thing I like about making brunch is that the ingredients are usually familiar and easy to find. And the recipes are relatively fast, so the dishes are on the table in much less time than other meals seem to take to prepare. Nothing braises for three hours, and there are no intricate sauces to slave over. For many of the recipes in this book, reading the recipe takes longer than the actual cooking!

If there's one thing I've learned from my decades of being a top pastry chef, it is this: It's not the difficult techniques or special equipment that makes things taste stellar—it's the ingredients and the way they are combined that make food so delicious. Using superb ingredients and combining them in innovative ways doesn't take any extra time or make cooking complicated. (In fact, the opposite is usually true.) Nowhere is this more evident than with the favorite recipes we all associate with brunch. Take my Hot Cocoa with Brown Sugar, for example: Making hot cocoa from scratch is incredibly easy, and simply swapping brown sugar for the usual granulated sugar gives it an unforgettable flavor. A big result that doesn't require any more time to make? That's my kind of cooking!

That's what separates the recipes in this book from the ho-hum standards you'll find in lots of places. So many of my favorites feature one or two unexpected ingredients that take them from good to great. French toast made with panettone instead of standard white bread is a decadent treat. Made with ciabatta and spiked with almonds, the same French toast concept is excellent in an entirely different way. And then there's freshly squeezed orange juice: It's terrific as is, but when you add lime juice and a splash of grenadine, it's over the top. If you like a side of bacon with your waffles, how about mixing a little bacon into your waffle batter for a sinfully good savory-sweet experience? Or eggs baked in ham cups in a muffin tin: a beautiful, delicious result for no more effort than your standard baked eggs.

Perhaps I appreciate brunch as much as I do because I've missed it so often, either because I had to be in the kitchen early, preparing the day's pastries, or because I was at work very late the night before and needed to sleep in the next morning. I sometimes have breakfast—or at least breakfast-type food—for dinner because it's so appealing to me. Breakfast is the most important meal of the day, so why not eat it anytime?

I got to enjoy breakfast a lot more often starting in 2006, when my partners and I opened Osteria di Tramonto, the first restaurant I've ever owned that serves breakfast. At the same time, we opened Gale's Coffee Bar, which serves breakfast food and beverages as well as all kinds of pastries. Both these places have been wonderful testing grounds for some of the recipes in this book. I get to see firsthand what foods people crave and regularly request in the morning.

Many of the breakfast and brunch items I make are inspired by wonderful bakeries and pastry shops in cities like Paris and San Francisco—places that understand the importance of a hot, milky cup of coffee served with warm buttery pastries and intensely flavored jams.

My husband, Jimmy, and I have a habit of searching for the best bakery in town wherever we go. We seek out small places that are adored by the locals and run with love, which is something I'd advise you to do near you—or wherever you travel. Once you've found your favorite local bakery, you can use it as a resource for putting together a basket of pastries for an informal get-together. In fact, if Jimmy were hosting brunch, he might do just that, though he would also have to leave with some doughnuts. He treats them as if they're one of the four food groups. I'd probably add a great coffee drink—maybe Iced Coffee with Cinnamon-Coffee Ice Cubes if it is summer—and perhaps some homemade preserves, like Apricot Ginger Jam. When the occasion calls for something more festive, turn to recipes such as Spinach and Cheddar Soufflé or Poached Salmon with Cucumber Yogurt. You can make one special dish the centerpiece of the meal, or you can create a beautiful buffet from an assortment of sweet and savory recipes. I'm getting hungry just thinking about all these great brunch foods!

From omelets to pancakes and waffles, there are tons of variations on all kinds of brunch basics in this book—as well as recipes for muffins, scones, salads, soups, and so much more. I encourage you to play with the recipes and try your own variations too. Because if eating and hosting brunch are about having a good time, making brunch should be a lot of fun too!

WHITE HOT CHOCOLATE WITH ORANGE

DRINKS

ICED COFFEE WITH CINNAMON-COFFEE ICE CUBES

THAI ICED COFFEE

CHAI TEA

FROZEN LATTE

HOT COCOA WITH BROWN SUGAR

WHITE HOT CHOCOLATE WITH ORANGE

BANANA-RASPBERRY SMOOTHIE

PINEAPPLE-BLUEBERRY SMOOTHIE

RASPBERRY LEMONADE

INFUSED LEMONADE

ORANGE-LIME JUICE WITH GRENADINE

TANGERINE–PINK GRAPEFRUIT JUICE

CHAMPAGNE AND CRANBERRY WITH MINT

CHAMPAGNE PIMM'S CUP

GALE'S 3-ALARM BLOODY MARY

ICED COFFEE
WITH CINNAMON-COFFEE ICE CUBES

SERVES 4

The thing about iced coffee that always frustrates me is that it gets watered down as the ice melts. Not with this version! Using ice cubes made of coffee means there's no dilution. Yes, you do have to plan ahead and make the cubes in advance, but they are a great place to funnel leftover coffee: Whenever you don't finish a pot, instead of dumping it down the drain, use it to make coffee ice cubes.

½ cup ground coffee, preferably light roast

½ cup whole milk

Cinnamon-Coffee Ice Cubes (page 18)

Sugar, preferably raw sugar

4 cinnamon sticks (optional)

Brew a batch of coffee using the ground coffee and 4 cups water. Once the coffee is brewed, mix in the milk. Place 3 or 4 cinnamon-coffee ice cubes in each of 4 glasses. Pour the milky coffee over the ice cubes and sweeten with sugar to taste. Garnish each glass with a cinnamon stick, if desired.

CINNAMON-COFFEE ICE CUBES

MAKES 12 TO 16 CUBES

¼ cup ground coffee, preferably dark roast

2 cinnamon sticks or 1 teaspoon ground cinnamon

At least a day before you want to serve iced coffee, brew a small batch of coffee, adding the cinnamon sticks or ground cinnamon to the filter, or to the press pot, with the ground coffee and 2 cups water. Let cool slightly. Then pour the cinnamon-flavored coffee into an ice cube tray and freeze overnight.

THE BEST BREW

COFFEE: You *can* get a good cup of coffee at home, especially if you keep a few things in mind. Buy your coffee in bean form and grind the beans right before you brew. Store the beans in an airtight container in a cool, dry, dark place (moisture, heat, and light can all interfere with coffee's flavor). Unless you won't be using your coffee beans for weeks and weeks, do not keep them in the freezer, as condensation can develop if they are exposed to warmth when you take them out of the freezer. Grind the beans fine for espresso and a bit coarser for French press or automatic drip. Measure carefully—a good place to start is 2 tablespoons of ground coffee for every 6 ounces of water. You can adjust that amount according to your personal taste, of course.

TEA: As with coffee, storage is important for tea. Keep your tea in an airtight container, in a cool (not refrigerated), dark, dry place. Start with cold water and bring it to a rolling boil for black and herbal teas; for more delicate green and white teas, heat the water to just under the boiling point. Pour the water from your kettle over tea leaves in a warmed teapot. If you're using loose-leaf tea (which generally offers better flavor than tea bags), use 1 teaspoon of tea for the pot and 1 teaspoon of tea per cup of water. Put the tea in a tea ball or infuser if you don't want to have to strain the tea into cups. Steep tea for 3 to 5 minutes, according to taste. Once the tea has steeped, it's best to remove the tea leaves from the pot to halt further steeping and prevent the tea from becoming bitter.

THAI
ICED COFFEE

SERVES 4

Some recipes for Thai iced coffee call for ingredients beyond what I use here, such as almond extract or anise. But for me, it's all about the creamy texture, with a touch of the exotic from cardamom, all cooled over ice. If you're buying whole cardamom pods, you have a choice: green cardamom gives a grassy flavor, whereas white cardamom is more refined tasting and almost sweet. For even more flavor, you can roast them in the oven or toss them in a sauté pan first. Ground cardamom is fine too, as long as it's fresh. Made with sweetened condensed milk, this coffee is really rich, and a little goes a long way. Think about serving it in little juice glasses or shot glasses and garnishing them with tiny umbrellas—and maybe using Cinnamon Coffee Ice Cubes (opposite).

½ cup ground coffee, preferably medium roast

2 teaspoons ground cardamom or 4 cardamom pods, crushed

4 teaspoons sugar, or more to taste

Ice cubes

½ cup sweetened condensed milk

Mix the coffee grounds with the cardamom, and brew the coffee with 4 cups water as you normally would. Stir in the sugar, and let the coffee cool slightly while you get the glasses ready. Fill 4 highball or tall glasses with ice. Pour the sweetened coffee over the ice. Pour 2 tablespoons sweetened condensed milk into each glass and do not stir—let it cascade down into the glass. Serve immediately.

CHAI TEA

SERVES 4

My neighbor Munisha had twin girls a week before I did, and though we had never met, we both soon noticed that our lights were on at the same times in the middle of the night as we spent sleepless hours tending to our infants. We got in touch by phone at first, and bonded through that tough first year. By year two we had finally met in person and started having dinner together. Our first meal at their home was a beautiful traditional Indian meal with a soothing finale of chai tea, which is tea flavored with spices, sweetened, and simmered with milk. It's a delicious alternative to coffee at brunch.

2 whole cloves

4 cardamom pods, crushed, or 2 teaspoons ground cardamom

½ cinnamon stick or ⅛ teaspoon ground cinnamon

1 slice fresh ginger or ⅛ teaspoon ground ginger

4 teaspoons Darjeeling or other black tea leaves

1 tablespoon dark brown sugar

1 cup whole milk

In a medium saucepan, combine 4 cups water with the cloves, cardamom, cinnamon, and ginger and bring to a boil over medium-high heat. Turn the heat off and add the tea, letting it steep for about 3 minutes. Add the brown sugar and milk, and simmer on low heat for 2 to 3 minutes (do not boil), stirring to dissolve the sugar. Strain the liquid into a container with a spout, and pour into teacups. Serve hot.

FROZEN LATTE

SERVES 4

This frothy, icy, milky drink is a good wake-up call! It's also satisfying and refreshing. For a more intense, ultra-caffeinated experience, use coffee ice cubes instead of plain ones. This recipe makes 6-ounce servings; if you want bigger drinks, double the recipe. You can use skim milk, whole milk, or cream depending on how indulgent you want to be. If you have a favorite flavored coffee, feel free to try it in this recipe.

4 shots (¾ cup) extra-strong
   brewed espresso

2 cups milk

⅛ teaspoon almond extract

1 tablespoon sugar

2 cups ice cubes

Combine the espresso, milk, almond extract, sugar, and ice in a blender and blend for about 30 seconds, until smooth but still icy. Serve immediately.

HOT COCOA
WITH BROWN SUGAR

SERVES 4

In the U.S., hot cocoa tends to be an after-school, after-skating, or evening indulgence. When I lived in France, it was breakfast—and what a nice way to start the day. The French understand the value of chocolate in the morning, and they make it carefully, with top-quality ingredients: the best cocoa, and whole milk instead of water. It's an excellent treat *whenever* you crave it. I make hot cocoa with brown sugar because it gives a warm, caramelized flavor, almost like toasted marshmallows. Needless to say, it's great topped with Homemade Marshmallows (opposite).

4 cups whole milk

¼ cup unsweetened cocoa powder

½ cup packed light brown sugar

¼ teaspoon pure vanilla extract

Whipped cream, for garnish

Chocolate shavings, for garnish

Pour the milk into a saucepan and heat to a simmer over medium heat.

Stir the cocoa powder and brown sugar together. A couple teaspoons at a time, stir about 2 tablespoons of the hot milk into the cocoa mixture to make a smooth paste. Add the cocoa paste to the milk in the saucepan and simmer for 2 minutes; do not let it boil. Remove from the heat and stir in the vanilla.

Pour into small mugs and add a dollop of whipped cream and a sprinkling of chocolate shavings on top of each. Serve immediately.

HOMEMADE MARSHMALLOWS

MAKES ABOUT 20 MARSHMALLOWS

- ¼ cup light corn syrup
- ¾ cup sugar
- 2 large egg whites
- 1 tablespoon powdered gelatin
- ¼ teaspoon pure vanilla extract
  Cornstarch, for dusting

NOTE: *To give the marsh-mallows a different flavor, replace the vanilla extract with lemon, mint, orange, or anise extract.*

Combine ¼ cup water with the corn syrup and sugar in a saucepan fitted with a candy thermometer. Bring to a boil and cook until the mixture reaches the "soft-ball" stage, or about 235 degrees.

Meanwhile, whip the egg whites on medium-high speed until soft peaks form (once they form, turn the mixer down to low and let it run until the syrup is ready). Sprinkle the gelatin over 2 tablespoons cold water in a bowl and let it dissolve.

When the syrup reaches 235 degrees, remove it from the heat, add the gelatin, and mix by swirling the pan gently. With the mixer on low speed, pour the syrup in a stream into the whipped egg whites. Add the vanilla and whip on medium-high speed until stiff peaks form, 3 to 5 minutes.

Line a baking sheet with parchment paper. Spread the mixture out on the paper and let it cool for at least 2 hours. Then cut it into 1-inch cubes and dust the cubes with cornstarch to keep them from sticking together. Store in an airtight container for up to 5 days.

WHITE HOT CHOCOLATE
WITH ORANGE

SERVES 4

White chocolate is very sweet and gentle, so it's best when complemented with a dash of something to enhance the flavor and cut the sweetness. A subtle touch of tart citrus is perfect. While white chocolate isn't my favorite ingredient, everyone in my family loves it. And I must admit, I do have fond memories of it. When I was growing up, I loved the white chocolate almond bark from Marshall Field's—sampling a food that seemed at the time to be so special and elegant was part of my becoming a gourmand.

3½ cups milk

½ cup heavy cream

Six 1 x 3-inch strips orange peel

8 ounces white chocolate, chopped

1 teaspoon almond extract

Combine the milk, cream, and orange peel in a medium saucepan and heat over medium-high heat, stirring occasionally, until boiling. Add the white chocolate and whisk until it has melted. Whisk in the almond extract and remove the orange peel. Reserve two of the orange peels and cut them into ¼-inch-wide strips. Ladle the white hot chocolate into mugs, garnish with the orange strips, and serve immediately.

VARIATION

WHITE HOT CHOCOLATE WITH MINT

Replace the orange peel with 8 mint leaves for infusing the milk and cream, plus another 4 mint leaves (1 for each cup) to replace the orange peel garnish, and replace the almond extract with 1 teaspoon vanilla extract. Follow the instructions above.

BANANA-RASPBERRY
SMOOTHIE

SERVES 1 TO 2

When I make smoothies, I use frozen fruit instead of ice cubes to make them frosty, because ice cubes can water down the flavor. In my freezer I keep what I call "smoothie kits" so my kids can make them anytime. When fruit starts to look like it's a little too ripe to eat fresh, but it's full of flavor, I cut it up, place it in a resealable plastic bag, and freeze it—it can keep for up to 3 months this way. I often combine two or three types of fruit per bag so each one is different and a surprise. Then I (or my kids) just empty the bag into the blender; add fruit juice, yogurt, or apple juice concentrate; and blend. Try this banana-raspberry version, or my Pineapple-Blueberry Smoothie (opposite), and then start inventing your own combinations. This recipe makes enough for 1 to 2 people who want generous servings; sometimes I make it and fill 4 to 6 shot glasses with a few sips to accompany brunch.

1 banana, sliced, preferably frozen

½ cup frozen raspberries

½ cup plain yogurt

½ cup orange juice

Combine the bananas, raspberries, yogurt, and orange juice in a blender and blend until smooth yet icy. Serve immediately.

PINEAPPLE-BLUEBERRY
SMOOTHIE

SERVES 1 TO 2

Pineapple is one of the few fruits I'll buy canned—it's lower in acid and has a milder flavor than fresh pineapple, so it works well in this smoothie, which is sweetened only by real fruit and apple juice concentrate. If you can find frozen pineapple, you can use that instead.

2 cups pineapple chunks, preferably frozen

1 cup frozen blueberries

½ cup frozen apple juice concentrate

½ cup plain yogurt

2 fresh mint leaves

Combine the pineapple, blueberries, apple juice concentrate, yogurt, and mint leaves in a blender and blend until smooth. Serve immediately.

RASPBERRY
LEMONADE

SERVES 4

I love taking everyday favorites and turning them into something special without much work. Simply adding a splash of fruit puree reinvents classic lemonade. To make it a little exotic, you could replace the raspberry puree with passion fruit puree, which is sometimes available in the international food section at supermarkets or at gourmet grocery stores.

1 cup fresh lemon juice

½ cup sugar

1 tablespoon strained raspberry puree (fresh or frozen)

Ice cubes

In a bowl, whisk 2 cups water with the lemon juice, sugar, and raspberry puree until the sugar is dissolved. Fill glasses half-full with ice, and pour the lemonade over the ice to chill it. Or chill the mixture in the refrigerator until you're ready to serve it.

INFUSED
LEMONADE

SERVES 4

This lemonade is just as easy to make as Raspberry Lemonade (page 29), but you do have to make it a day in advance so the flavor of the ginger has time to seep into the lemonade. You could replace the ginger with 1 tablespoon dried lavender blossoms, 1 tablespoon fresh mint leaves, 1 teaspoon fresh thyme leaves, or 1 teaspoon fresh rosemary for a different flavor; these will need to infuse overnight too.

1 cup fresh lemon juice

½ cup sugar

1 tablespoon minced fresh ginger

Ice cubes

In a bowl, whisk 2 cups water with the lemon juice, sugar, and ginger until the sugar is dissolved. Let sit overnight in the refrigerator to infuse the ginger flavor.

Just before serving, whisk again and then strain. Fill glasses halfway with ice and pour the lemonade over the ice.

ORANGE-LIME JUICE
WITH GRENADINE

SERVES 4

This juice is refreshing and fantastic to serve with eggs—I think eggs are best when accompanied by citrus juice to cleanse the palate. Grenadine, a red syrup that was originally made from pomegranate juice and sugar, gives it a pretty blush. This juice is delicious made with either regular limes or Key limes. Float a few pomegranate seeds in each glass for a fun garnish.

4 oranges

2 limes or 4 Key limes

2 teaspoons grenadine or pomegranate juice

Slice the oranges and limes in half and juice them. Combine the juices in a pitcher, and chill if desired. Pour the juice mixture into juice glasses. Then, just before serving, slowly pour ½ teaspoon grenadine into each glass so there's a ribbon of pink in the juice. Have your guests stir the juice with straws to turn it pink.

FLAVORED ICE CUBES

Make any drink more fun and festive by chilling it with flavored ice cubes. I always have some kind of fun cube in my freezer. You can add strips of lemon, orange, or lime peel to water in an ice tray before it freezes, or add whole berries or herbs. When the cubes melt, they leave a little surprise in the drink. You can also make ice cubes out of liquids other than water, such as lemonade or tea or white grape juice. Dress up store-bought OJ with ruby-colored ice cubes made from cranberry juice. They're pretty and require almost no work.

TANGERINE–PINK
GRAPEFRUIT JUICE

SERVES 4

One of the things kids love helping with in the kitchen is juicing citrus fruits. I have a tabletop electric juicer, and my son, Gio, loves to use it. I put a bowl of cut citrus next to him and he has them juiced in no time. It's fun to combine juice from two or three different fruits. In this combination, the sweetness of the tangerine mellows out the tartness of the grapefruit. You could also use tangelos, mandarin oranges, satsumas, or blood oranges with the grapefruit.

4 tangerines

2 pink grapefruits

Ice cubes

4 fresh mint leaves

Slice the tangerines and grapefruits in half and juice them. Combine the juice in a pitcher, and chill if desired. Serve in juice glasses with a little ice and a mint leaf tucked into each glass.

CHAMPAGNE
AND CRANBERRY WITH MINT

I love the contrast of blushing cranberry-colored Champagne and bright green mint leaves in this celebratory drink. When our friends the Katzes come to visit during the holidays, we try to have a signature drink to mark the occasion. This was last year's gem, which I especially love because it features Champagne. I think Champagne goes with any time of day, and any occasion. Like a strand of pearls, it's always appropriate. Plus, it's a beautiful thing to serve to guests. You don't need to serve this in flutes (though that would be gorgeous), but do serve it in something tall and thin so you can watch the bubbles ascend. Use a brut (dry) Champagne if you like your cocktails crisp, or a demi-sec (literally, half-dry) if you prefer something a little sweeter.

½ cup sugar, plus more for the glass rims

1 strip orange zest, removed with a vegetable peeler and cut into 6 strips

1½ cups (6 ounces) fresh cranberries

4 to 6 large fresh mint sprigs

1 (750-ml) bottle Champagne, chilled

In a small saucepan, combine 1 cup water, the sugar, and the orange zest and bring to a boil over medium-high heat. Boil for 3 minutes. Then add the cranberries and turn the heat down to medium. Let simmer until the berries pop open, about 4 minutes. Let cool in the pan for about 5 minutes, then puree well in a blender or food processor. Chill the cranberry puree until ready to use (up to 1 week in an airtight container).

To serve, dip the rim of your glass or flute (just the first ⅛ inch) into the cranberry puree, and then dip it into sugar to sugar-coat the rim. Spoon 2 tablespoons of the cranberry puree into each glass. Stick a mint sprig in each glass, and then pour in enough Champagne to fill each glass halfway. Let the Champagne settle before filling again, almost to the rim. Serve immediately.

CHAMPAGNE
PIMM'S CUP

SERVES 4

A Pimm's Cup is a classic English cocktail, and I drank plenty of them during the three years I lived in England. The original recipe called for Pimm's No. 1, a gin-based spirit flavored with fruit that dates back to the 1820s, along with lemonade, sliced fruit, and fresh mint; 7-Up and ginger ale are common add-ins. Now there are many, many variations, using Pimm's No. 1 through No. 6. Because I love Champagne, I wanted to include it in my version of a Pimm's Cup, which is less sweet than the original but still has plenty of flavors and textures going on. This is refreshing in the spring and summer. In the fall and around the holidays, you can toss in a few cranberries for a festive splash of color.

1 cup Pimm's No. 1

1 green apple, cored and cut into thin slices

8 orange slices, each ¼ inch thick

8 lemon slices, each ¼ inch thick

4 cucumber spears (do not peel), 3 to 4 inches long

4 fresh mint sprigs

1 (750-ml) bottle Champagne, chilled

8 cranberries (optional)

Into each of 4 highball or straight tall glasses, pour ¼ cup Pimm's No. 1. Add 2 apple slices, 2 orange slices, 2 lemon slices, a cucumber spear, and a mint sprig to each glass. (If possible, the mint and cucumber should stick out of the top of the glass.) Fill each glass to the halfway point with Champagne, allow it to settle, and then fill it to the rim. Garnish with cranberries, if desired. Serve immediately.

GALE'S 3-ALARM
BLOODY MARY

SERVES 4

There are lots of variations on this daytime cocktail, which was invented in Paris in 1921. Some use lime juice, celery seed, chiles, black pepper, and Clamato juice (people say it's wonderful, but I'm sorry, the idea of clam liquid in my morning cocktail just doesn't appeal). Etiquette says the Bloody Mary should never be served after 6 p.m., so it's the perfect brunch accompaniment. I never feel entirely guilty starting the day with a Bloody Mary because it seems so healthy, with all the vegetables—almost like a salad. Make sure you use pure grated horseradish, not creamy style.

1 cup vodka

2 cups good-quality tomato juice

Juice of 2 lemons

1 tablespoon Worcestershire sauce

16 drops Tabasco sauce

¾ teaspoon celery salt

¾ teaspoon cayenne pepper

1 tablespoon prepared horseradish

Ice cubes

4 carrot sticks

4 celery sticks

4 lemon wedges

4 olives

In a pitcher, combine the vodka, tomato juice, lemon juice, Worcestershire, Tabasco, celery salt, cayenne, and horseradish with about 1 cup of ice and stir well. Strain into highball glasses over ice cubes. Garnish each glass with a carrot stick, a celery stick, a lemon wedge, and an olive on a toothpick.

STRATA 101

Brunch
BASICS

OMELET 101

STRATA 101

FRITTATA 101

QUICHE 101

CRÊPES 101

OMELET
101

Before you begin, know that cooking an omelet takes less time than reading the recipe for an omelet. They are very quick! So have everything ready to go when you start cooking. I prefer to make omelets in an 8-inch omelet pan or a sauté pan with curved edges to make them easier to get out of the pan. Use a nonstick pan if you have one, but make sure it's new or in good condition—no peeling or chipping, please. I like to beat eggs with a little water when making an omelet because it makes it easier to distribute them in the pan and cook them evenly. The eggs should be stirred at first to help them cook through; then at the last minute you should stop stirring to allow the omelet to set. Sometimes omelets are filled with added ingredients (an omelet is a great way to use up small amounts of leftover ingredients, from blanched asparagus to ratatouille) and sometimes they're served plain. Either way, when an omelet is done, traditionally you carefully roll it out of the pan onto a plate. My husband garnishes his omelets with ketchup (or "chupup," as our three-year-olds call it—he's got them doing it too), but only when I'm not around.

2 large eggs

2 pinches salt

2 grinds freshly ground black pepper

1 teaspoon unsalted butter

Filling ingredients (see Variations, page 42; optional)

In a mixing bowl, beat the eggs, 2 teaspoons water, the salt, and the pepper with a fork until the eggs are almost fully combined (a little white is okay), about 15 seconds.

Heat the butter in a nonstick omelet pan over medium-high heat until the butter foams. When it stops foaming, sauté any filling ingredients that need cooking first; then scrape them out of the pan into a bowl.

Pour the eggs into the pan and stir them gently with a wooden spoon (as if you're making scrambled eggs), folding the egg mixture over itself and allowing the uncooked egg to run under the cooked egg to help cook it through. Stop stirring just before the eggs are completely cooked (after 2 to 3 minutes), and use the back of the spoon to spread the eggs out evenly in the pan. Quickly add any filling ingredients as directed, and sprinkle with any cheese you might be using.

{CONTINUED ON PAGE 42}

(If adding cheese, cover the pan with a lid to melt the cheese.) Let the omelet cook for just 30 more seconds in the pan if you like your omelet light (1 more minute if you like it a little browned), then turn off the heat immediately.

To turn the omelet out of the pan, hold the pan handle in your left hand (assuming you are right-handed). Tilt the edge of the pan down slightly, right over your serving plate. Use a rubber spatula to roll the omelet out of the pan, starting at the top of the pan. (I draw a line with my spatula behind the omelet around the top edge, and it starts to roll down out of the pan until it falls in a roll onto the plate.) Serve immediately.

OMELET
VARIATIONS

The quantities listed for each variation are per individual omelet.
For more filling ideas, check out the variations for Strata 101 (page 46)
and Frittata 101 (page 50).

SPINACH, SHIITAKE, AND SWISS

Add 1 teaspoon olive oil to the 1 teaspoon butter in the pan and heat for about 1 minute. Add ¼ cup sliced fresh shiitake mushrooms and sauté them until tender, about 3 minutes. Add 1 cup whole-leaf spinach and cook for 1 minute, until wilted. Set aside. Stir the mixture into the omelet just before it sets, spreading it out evenly to set with the eggs. Sprinkle with ¼ cup grated Swiss cheese and finish the omelet as directed.

TRI-COLOR BELL PEPPER, HAM, AND CHEDDAR

Sauté 2 tablespoons chopped green bell pepper, 2 tablespoons chopped red bell pepper, and 2 tablespoons chopped yellow bell pepper in the butter until tender and slightly browned, about 3 minutes. Add ¼ cup cubed ham and cook for 30 seconds. Set aside. Stir the mixture into the omelet just before it sets, spreading it out evenly to set with the eggs. Sprinkle with ¼ cup grated cheddar cheese and finish the omelet as directed.

ITALIAN SPICY SALAMI, BROCCOLI RABE, AND MOZZARELLA

Mario Batali came to my restaurant several years ago for a dinner and book signing, and he brought us some of his own cured salami as a gift. I brought it home and my son, Gio, who was six at the time, just loved it and requested it in omelets constantly. When we ran out, Gio asked, "Mom, can you ask that cook Mario who works for you to make us some more of that great sausage?" He thought that since his mom is a chef and restaurant owner, everyone works for me, even Mario Batali!

Cook 2 to 3 spears broccoli rabe in boiling salted water for about 3 minutes, until crisp-tender, and set aside. Heat the omelet pan on medium heat and sauté 2 tablespoons julienned spicy Italian cured salami, preferably made by Mario Batali. (You don't need any butter or oil in the pan to sauté the salami; the heat will draw out some of the fat into the pan, which will make your omelet very tasty.) Set the salami aside. Lay the salami and broccoli rabe along the center of the omelet just before it sets. Sprinkle with ¼ cup cubed fresh mozzarella and finish the omelet as directed.

OVEN-ROASTED TOMATOES, SCALLION, AND GOAT CHEESE

Sauté the chopped white and green parts of 1 scallion in the butter for 1 to 2 minutes, until tender. Chop 4 quarters of Oven-Roasted Tomatoes (page 136) and add them to the pan, tossing for a minute until they are warm. Then add the eggs and proceed with the rest of the recipe, stirring the tomatoes and scallion into the eggs. Sprinkle ¼ cup goat cheese on at the end.

CAVIAR AND CRÈME FRAÎCHE

Cook a basic omelet (with no additional ingredients) so it's light, not browned (30 seconds at the end, not 1 minute), and roll the omelet out onto a serving plate. Use a sharp paring knife to make a deep slit in the top of the rolled omelet, and spoon in ¼ cup crème fraîche. Spoon 1 tablespoon caviar over the crème fraîche, and sprinkle the omelet with ¼ teaspoon finely chopped fresh chives. And then thank whomever you pray to for this wonderful gift!

STRATA
101

SERVES 8

Strata is the bread pudding of savory egg dishes. This super-easy treat generally includes cubes or slices of bread that have been soaked in custard, then baked in a casserole dish or a rectangular baking pan. This is a great make-ahead dish—it tastes best if you prepare it the day before and let it soak overnight before baking. Like many egg dishes, a strata can incorporate all sorts of different ingredients, so there's a lot of flexibility here.

5 cups cubed French bread (with crust)

Grated cheese (see Variations)

10 large eggs

1 quart whole milk

1 teaspoon dry mustard

1 teaspoon salt

Filling ingredients (see Variations, page 46)

Butter a 9x13-inch baking dish. Put the bread cubes in the dish and sprinkle them with the cheese. In a large bowl, whisk together the eggs, milk, mustard, and salt. Pour the egg mixture over the bread cubes. Sprinkle the filling ingredients over the egg mixture and fold them in gently. Cover, and chill for at least 4 hours and up to 24 hours.

Heat the oven to 350 degrees.

Uncover the baking dish and bake for 60 minutes, until the mixture has puffed up slightly and is golden brown on top, and the strata doesn't shimmy with uncooked custard when you shake the pan. Tent the dish with foil if the top is browning too quickly. Let cool for 5 minutes before serving. Serve by the spoonful, using a large serving spoon.

STRATA

VARIATIONS

BACON, CHEDDAR, MUSHROOM, AND TOMATO	Sprinkle 2 cups grated sharp cheddar cheese over the bread cubes. Distribute 1 cup crumbled cooked bacon (6 to 8 strips), 1 cup sautéed sliced white or shiitake mushrooms, and 1 cup chopped tomatoes over the egg mixture.
CHICKEN, BROCCOLI, CORN, CHILES, AND JACK	Sprinkle 2 cups grated Monterey Jack cheese over the bread cubes. Distribute 1 cup frozen corn kernels, 1 cup cooked broccoli florets, two 4.5-ounce cans (drained) chopped green chiles, and ½ cup shredded cooked chicken over the egg mixture.
HAM, SWISS, AND ASPARAGUS	Sprinkle 2 cups grated Swiss cheese over the bread cubes. Distribute 1 cup blanched asparagus pieces, 1 cup cubed ham, and ½ cup caramelized onions (see page 152) over the egg mixture.
FONTINA, SPINACH, SALAMI, AND ROASTED GARLIC	Sprinkle 2 cups Fontina cheese over the bread cubes. Distribute 1 cup frozen chopped spinach, 1 cup Italian salami (cut into matchsticks), and ½ cup roughly chopped roasted garlic cloves (see note, opposite) over the egg mixture.
VEGETABLE–BLUE CHEESE	Sprinkle 1 cup crumbled blue cheese over the bread cubes. Distribute 1 cup cooked cubed celery root, 1 cup sautéed sliced zucchini, and ½ cup sautéed sliced onions over the egg mixture.

ROASTING GARLIC

Heat the oven to 400 degrees. Place a square of foil, large enough to make a bundle around however many bulbs of garlic you plan to roast, on a work surface. Cut about ¼ inch off the top of the garlic bulbs and place them on the foil, cut side up. Sprinkle each bulb with about 1 teaspoon olive oil, and gather the foil to make a bundle. The bundle doesn't need to be airtight, but it should be gathered at the top. Roast for about 1 hour, until soft. Then remove the garlic from the oven and let it cool, still bundled up, for at least 10 minutes. Open up the bundle, separate the cloves, and peel them by popping the garlic out of the skins. The garlic cloves should be soft and golden brown. Roasted garlic keeps for up to a week in an airtight container in the refrigerator.

FRITTATA
101

A frittata is similar to an omelet, but it's crammed with more *stuff*. It generally includes eggs beaten with cream or milk, vegetables, meats, cheeses, and pasta cooked together in a frying pan to make a thick disk. The technique for making a frittata is similar to the one you'd use to make an omelet, but the added ingredients are stirred into the egg mixture before it is cooked, and the frittata is served as a whole disk, not rolled at the end, making it a great choice for those of us who fear omelet-rolling. I make my frittatas nice and thick so they can be cut into wedges, and I flip them onto a platter before serving to show the golden brown underside. A frittata is another great way to use up leftover bits of vegetables, meats, and cheese, so feel free to deviate from my suggestions, depending on what you have in your fridge.

6 eggs

¼ cup heavy cream or whole milk

¼ teaspoon salt

3 to 4 grinds freshly ground black pepper

1 tablespoon grated Parmesan cheese

Filling ingredients (see Variations, page 50; optional)

1 tablespoon unsalted butter

In a medium bowl, mix the eggs with a fork. Blend in the cream, salt, pepper, and Parmesan. Add any filling ingredients and stir together to blend.

In an 8-inch nonstick sauté pan, heat the butter over medium heat until it foams. Pour in the egg mixture and start to cook it. After about 2 minutes, stick a wooden spoon into the egg at the edge of the pan, lift up the cooked egg, and let some of the uncooked egg mixture seep underneath. Cook for 2 more minutes. Then insert the wooden spoon into the egg in the middle of the pan, making a hole in the cooked egg to let some of the uncooked egg seep under. Turn the heat down to low, place a rounded lid on the pan (make sure you allow room for the egg to puff up), and cook until the egg mixture is completely set, 5 to 10 minutes. Once the frittata is cooked all the way through, flip it out onto a serving platter, using a spatula or knife to loosen it from the pan and letting it fall onto the platter browned side up. Serve hot, cut into wedges.

FRITTATA
VARIATIONS

CHEDDAR, PANCETTA, AND SPINACH

Add ½ cup shredded cheddar cheese, ⅓ cup sautéed chopped pancetta (3 slices), ⅓ cup sautéed diced yellow bell pepper (½ pepper), ½ cup wilted chopped spinach, and 1 cup cooked spaghetti to the egg mixture. Serve the frittata with marinara sauce on the side.

SALAMI, POTATO, AND PESTO

Add ½ cup slivered Genoa salami (cut into matchsticks), 1½ cups cubed cooked potato (1 large russet, Idaho, or Yukon Gold), ½ cup halved cherry tomatoes, and ½ cup grated Provolone to the egg mixture. Serve the frittata with homemade pesto (page 139) or store-bought pesto drizzled over the wedges (thin the pesto with olive oil to make it pourable).

SALMON, SCALLION, AND GOAT CHEESE

Add 2 ounces chopped smoked or cured salmon, ¼ cup chopped scallions (white and green parts), ½ cup cooked broccoli florets, 1 cup cooked flat noodles, and ½ cup crumbled goat cheese to the egg mixture. Serve the frittata with sour cream on the side.

EDAMAME, ARTICHOKE, AND JACK

Add ½ cup shelled edamame, ⅓ cup sautéed diced red bell pepper (½ pepper), ½ cup chopped artichoke hearts, ½ cup thawed frozen corn kernels, 1 cup cooked spinach fettuccine, and ½ cup shredded Monterey Jack cheese to the egg mixture.

PEAS, HAM, AND PROVOLONE

Add ½ cup blanched peas, ½ cup cubed ham, 1 tablespoon chopped flat-leaf parsley leaves, 1 cup cooked 1-inch tubetti pasta, and ½ cup grated Provolone cheese to the egg mixture.

QUICHE
101

A quiche is a baked custard pie with a simple bottom crust and no top crust, meant to be cut into wedges and served. You can add whatever you like to the custard: vegetables, meat, and definitely cheese. I try to add ingredients that have a lot of flavor, don't contain too much liquid, and will benefit from being caressed by a warm, mellow custard (wouldn't we all benefit from that?). You can make quiches in a French tart pan, in an American pie pan, or in mini pans so they can be devoured in a bite or two. You can even make them in a store-bought frozen pie crust, truth be told. Quiches are great brunch food because they can be served hot or made in advance and served at room temperature.

FOR THE CRUST

- 2¼ cups sifted all-purpose flour, plus more for rolling
- 1 teaspoon salt
- 1 teaspoon sugar
- ¾ cup (1½ sticks) cold butter, cut into pieces
- ¼ cup ice water
- 1 teaspoon red wine vinegar

FOR THE FILLING

- 3 large eggs
- 1 cup heavy cream
- 1 cup whole milk
- Shredded cheese (see Variations)
- Filling ingredients (see Variations, page 54)
- 1 teaspoon chopped fresh parsley
- 3 gratings whole nutmeg or 3 pinches ground nutmeg
- 6 dashes Tabasco or other hot sauce

To make the crust, mix the flour, salt, and sugar for 1 minute in the bowl of an electric mixer fitted with the paddle attachment or in a food processor. Add the butter and mix just until you have a crumbly, sandy mixture. You should still be able to see the pieces of butter.

In a small bowl, stir the ice water and vinegar together. With the mixer running at medium speed, drizzle in the water-vinegar mixture and mix just until a dough forms. You should still see small bits of butter.

{CONTINUED ON PAGE 53}

Turn the dough out onto a floured work surface and shape it into a disk. Wrap it tightly in plastic wrap and refrigerate it for at least 30 minutes. (At this point you can refrigerate the dough for up to 48 hours, or freeze it for up to 1 month, before using. If frozen, let it thaw in the refrigerator overnight before rolling it out.)

When you're ready to roll out the dough, if it's been chilled overnight, let it warm up for about 5 minutes at room temperature. Dust a work surface with a few tablespoons of flour. Set a 9-inch pie or tart pan nearby. Sprinkle a little flour on top of the dough and start rolling it outward from the center with quick, light strokes. Don't worry if the edges split a bit; concentrate on getting a good circle going from the center. Lift up and rotate the dough a quarter turn every minute or so to help ensure even rolling. If it gets sticky, sprinkle on a bit more flour, put it on a baking sheet and chill it in the refrigerator for 15 minutes to firm up. Keep rolling until the circle is at least 2 inches larger than your pie pan.

To transfer the crust to the pan, it's easiest to roll the finished crust onto the rolling pin and then gently unroll it in the pan. Make sure the dough settles completely into the pan. Don't stretch and press the dough into the corners; stretched dough may shrink back when you bake it. Instead, lift the edges of the crust to let it settle into the corners. If the dough tears a bit, don't be concerned; you can patch it with scraps (wet the scraps if necessary to help them stick). Use scissors or a sharp knife to trim the dough to within ¾ inch of the rim.

Working around the edge, turn the crust under itself (*not* under the rim of the pan) to make a thick edge. To crimp the edge of the crust, use the forefinger of one hand to push the thick dough rim *outward* while pushing *inward* with the thumb and forefinger of the other hand, so that they intersect in a V with the dough in between. Repeat around the edge to make a rickack (zigzag) pattern.

Cover the crust and chill it for 30 minutes, or up to 2 days, before filling.

Heat the oven to 375 degrees.

To make the filling, whisk together the eggs, cream, and milk in a medium bowl until smooth. Stir in the cheese, the filling ingredients, and the parsley, nutmeg, and Tabasco.

Place the chilled pie crust on a baking sheet, and pour the egg mixture into it. Bake for 50 to 60 minutes, until the quiche is slightly puffed and golden brown on top. Check for doneness by sticking a knife into the custard: It should come out clean, though it may look wet. Serve hot or at room temperature, cut into wedges.

QUICHE
VARIATIONS

ASPARAGUS, BLACK TRUFFLE, AND GOUDA

Stir 1 cup blanched asparagus pieces, 1 thinly sliced fresh or canned black truffle, and 2 cups grated Gouda into the egg mixture.

SPINACH, SHIITAKE, SWISS, AND FETA

Stir 1 cup thawed frozen chopped spinach, 1 cup sautéed fresh sliced shiitake mushrooms, 1 cup grated Swiss cheese, and 1 cup crumbled feta cheese into the egg mixture.

HAM, CARAMELIZED ONION, AND GRUYÈRE

Stir 1 cup cubed ham, ½ cup caramelized onions (see page 152), and 2 cups grated Gruyère cheese into the egg mixture.

OVEN-ROASTED TOMATO, NIÇOISE OLIVE, MOZZARELLA, AND GOAT CHEESE

Stir 16 pieces Oven-Roasted Tomatoes (page 136), 16 pitted Niçoise olives (halved), 1 cup grated mozzarella, and 1 cup crumbled goat cheese into the egg mixture.

BROCCOLI, BACON, AND BLUE CHEESE

Stir 1 cup cooked broccoli florets, ½ cup crumbled cooked bacon (3 to 4 strips), and 1 cup crumbled blue cheese into the egg mixture.

CRÊPES
101

MAKES ABOUT 12 CRÊPES; SERVES 4

A crêpe is a very thin, tender pancake that can be a sweet treat or a savory dish depending on what you fill it with. My mother made crêpes often. She served them for breakfast, either plain with a sprinkling of confectioners' sugar or filled with something sweet, or she rolled them around a savory filling for a quick lunch or a light dinner. She called them blintzes, but really they're the same thing. I've included both sweet and savory fillings in the variations on page 56. If you try making crêpes once, you'll see how easy they are, and I bet you'll start making them all the time. You can even make them in advance! Plan on about 3 crêpes per person.

4 large eggs	1 cup all-purpose flour
1 cup whole milk	Unsalted butter
½ teaspoon salt	Confectioners' sugar or fillings (see Variations, page 56)
1 teaspoon sugar	

In a medium bowl, whisk together the eggs and milk. Whisk in the salt, sugar, and flour until well combined but still a bit lumpy; then set the batter aside for 30 minutes to let it tenderize. Whisk the batter one more time before cooking.

In a nonstick 8-inch skillet, melt about ½ teaspoon butter over medium heat. When the butter foams, use your left hand (assuming you're right-handed) to pour or ladle in about 3 tablespoons of the batter into the center of the pan. Immediately lift the pan from the burner with your right hand and swirl it so the batter coats the bottom of the pan. Replace the pan on the burner and cook the crêpe until the batter is just set and the underside is lightly browned, 1 to 2 minutes. Using a spatula or your fingers, flip the crêpe and cook it until the other side is lightly browned, 30 seconds to 1 minute. Transfer the crêpe to a platter. Repeat with the remaining batter, stacking the cooked crêpes on top of one another. (You can store them in the refrigerator for up to 2 days, stacked and covered, or in the freezer for up to 1 month, rolled up or stacked with layers of wax paper in between.)

Serve warm or at room temperature, sprinkled with confectioners' sugar; or add a filling to the crêpes and roll them up like cigars.

CRÊPE
VARIATIONS

SWEET PEACH Divide about 3 cups ricotta cheese, 1½ cups thin slices of peaches, and ¼ cup honey among the crêpes: Spread each crêpe with about ¼ cup ricotta cheese, add 3 to 4 peach slices, and drizzle with about 1 teaspoon honey.

BANANA-NUTELLA Divide about 1½ cups Nutella or Chocolate-Hazelnut Spread (page 190), 1½ cups sliced bananas, and about 3 cups whipped cream among the crêpes: Spread each crêpe with about 2 tablespoons Nutella, add several banana slices, and then spread with about ¼ cup whipped cream.

PINEAPPLE Divide about 1½ cups sour cream, 3 cups fresh pineapple chunks, and ½ cup brown sugar among the crêpes: Spread each crêpe with about 2 tablespoons sour cream, add ¼ cup pineapple chunks, and sprinkle with 2 teaspoons light brown sugar.

ROASTED RED PEPPER AND FETA Divide about 2¼ cups roasted red pepper strips and 1½ cups crumbled feta cheese among the crêpes: Fill each crêpe with about 3 tablespoons pepper strips and 1 to 2 tablespoons crumbled feta.

SWEET POTATO Divide about 3 cups warm mashed sweet potatoes and 2 tablespoons chopped fresh rosemary among the crêpes: Spread each crêpe with about ¼ cup warm mashed sweet potato and sprinkle with ½ teaspoon rosemary.

ASPARAGUS WITH POACHED EGGS AND PARMESAN

More
EGGS

SALAMI AND **SCRAMBLED EGGS**

BREAKFAST BURRITOS

CUCURUMAO

VOODOO EGGS **IN TOAST**

TORTA RUSTICA

BAKED EGGS IN **HAM CUPS**

BACON AND EGG SALAD SANDWICHES

FRIED **MATZOH**

SPINACH AND CHEDDAR SOUFFLÉ

ASPARAGUS WITH POACHED EGGS AND PARMESAN

CODDLED **EGGS**

SALAMI
AND SCRAMBLED EGGS

SERVES 4

When I was a kid, a big splurge in my house was a whole kosher all-beef salami. (Chicago is famous for this stuff—both Vienna Beef and Best's Kosher call Chicago home. So does Oscar Mayer, but they're not kosher.) We would devour half of it with brick cheese and spicy mustard on soft Danish rye bread from Deerfield Bakery. The other half had to wait until Sunday morning, when Mom made salami and eggs. I still love the salty, chewy caramelization that happens in the skillet as the salami wedges cook, rendering fat in which to scramble the eggs. I serve these eggs with rye toast and glasses of citrus juice, which cuts through the richness of the dish and cleanses the palate between bites.

Six ¼-inch-thick slices kosher all-beef salami

8 large eggs

Freshly ground black pepper

Quarter the salami slices to make wedges. Sauté the salami wedges in a skillet over medium heat, stirring and cooking the wedges on both sides until they are slightly browned on the edges and have released some of their fat, 1 to 2 minutes.

Meanwhile, break the eggs into a bowl and mix them with a fork. Mix in 1 tablespoon water and season with pepper. You probably won't need any salt, as the salami provides plenty of saltiness.

Pour the egg mixture into the hot skillet, over the salami, and stir to cook the eggs and to break them up a bit, as you would with scrambled eggs. When the eggs are cooked through but not overcooked (after 2 to 3 minutes), dish spoonfuls of egg and salami onto warm plates.

BREAKFAST
BURRITOS

MAKES 8 BURRITOS; SERVES 4

Breakfast burritos have become a staple in my life. Early in the day in restaurant kitchens, line cooks and sous-chefs often make breakfast burritos for the staff. Not only are they delicious, they are an ideal make-ahead food—you can prepare these toasty bundles an hour or two ahead. And they're portable too—so you can make them for a breakfast or brunch on the go, such as a morning picnic or tailgate.

8 large eggs

Salt and freshly ground black pepper

1 teaspoon unsalted butter

Eight 6-inch flour tortillas

8 slices ham

1 cup grated cheddar or Monterey Jack cheese

1 avocado, sliced

½ cup salsa

½ cup sour cream

In a medium bowl, beat the eggs and 4 teaspoons water together with a fork. Season with salt and pepper. Melt the butter in a skillet, add the eggs, and scramble them over medium heat, stirring with a wooden spoon until they are cooked through but not overcooked, 2 to 3 minutes.

Meanwhile, warm the tortillas, one at a time, on both sides over an open flame, on an electric burner, or on a hot griddle just until they start to pick up some color, 5 to 10 seconds per side (keep your eye on them); or warm them in the microwave. Pile the tortillas on a plate to keep them warm and flexible.

To assemble the burritos, place a tortilla on a work surface and layer it with a slice of ham, then 2 tablespoons grated cheese, then an avocado slice, then 1 tablespoon each of salsa and sour cream, and then some of the scrambled eggs. Roll up the burrito and wrap it in foil, twisting the ends of the foil to enclose the burrito. Repeat with the remaining tortillas.

Place the burritos in a toaster oven or in a regular oven at 350 degrees to warm them all the way through and melt the cheese, or simply keep them warm in a 250-degree oven until ready to eat. To serve, untwist the foil at one end and peel it back to expose the burrito.

CUCURUMAO

SERVES 3 TO 4

This recipe comes from my husband's namesake grandfather, Jimmy Galati (whose real name was Vincenzo, but there were too many Vinnys at the Brooklyn shipyard where he worked, so everyone called him Jimmy). We think he made up the dish out of ingredients available in the kitchen one day when he was home alone with his children. They gobbled it down, so he made it again and again after that. The dish is similar to something I've seen called "Eggs in Purgatory," but Jimmy was born in Sicily, and the name he gave it comes from a Sicilian dialect. The spelling is odd, the pronunciation even odder: goo-ga-de-mow.

2 tablespoons olive oil

1 medium onion, chopped, or 2 cloves garlic, minced

2 pinches red pepper flakes (optional)

One 28-ounce can whole or crushed Italian plum tomatoes, with juice

Salt and freshly ground black pepper

1 to 2 pinches sugar, to taste (optional)

4 fresh basil leaves, torn

6 large eggs

Grated Parmesan cheese, for sprinkling (optional)

1 loaf crusty Italian bread

Heat the olive oil in a large sauté pan over medium heat. Add the onion and sauté until it is translucent and slightly golden, about 4 minutes. (If you're using garlic instead of onion, sauté it for 1 minute.) If you want this to be spicy, add the red pepper flakes and sauté for 1 more minute. Add the tomatoes (if whole, crush them with the back of a spoon). Cook until the mixture is fairly thick, about 20 minutes; then season it with salt and pepper. Taste the tomato sauce, and if you think you'd like it to be a little sweeter, add the sugar. Stir in the basil leaves.

Make six depressions in the tomato sauce with the back of a large spoon, and break 1 egg into each depression. Baste the eggs with a little tomato sauce, cover the pan, and cook over medium heat to poach the eggs, about 4 minutes.

Carefully divide the eggs and sauce among 3 or 4 bowls. Top with grated Parmesan, if desired (the original recipe didn't call for cheese, but my son, Gio, loves it this way), and serve with thick slices of bread.

VOODOO EGGS
IN TOAST

SERVES 4

Have I mentioned the love affair I'm having with my griddle? It's the greatest thing ever. It straddles two burners, and I can cook loads of pancakes at the same time, four or even six grilled cheese sandwiches all at once, and this dish—no sweat. The name comes from the single yolk in the center of the toast, which looks a little bit like an evil eye. I am always looking for new ways to cook eggs for my son (no cold cereal for this kid . . . he eats only hot cooked breakfasts), and this is one of his favorites. I cut a hole out of the center of a large piece of bread and crack the egg right into it. It's a simple and fun brunch dish that kids always love.

4 large slices white Italian bread

About 2 tablespoons unsalted butter, at room temperature

4 large eggs

Salt and freshly ground black pepper

Heat a griddle or a very large, flat frying pan over medium heat. Butter the bread slices on both sides, place them on the griddle, and toast them on one side. Then remove them from the griddle and cut a 3-inch hole in the center of each toast, reserving the disk you cut out. Return the bread to the griddle, toasted side down, and break an egg into the hole in each slice. Sprinkle the egg with salt and pepper, and cook until the white is firm and cooked but the yolk is still runny, 3 to 4 minutes. Place the cut-out disks on the griddle to toast the second side. Serve each egg-filled toast with a round disk of toast leaning against the side.

TORTA RUSTICA

MAKES ONE 9-INCH TORTA; SERVES 6 TO 8

The first torta I tasted was one from La Brea Bakery in Los Angeles, and it was amazing. I decided to look it up, and I learned that this genre of savory pastry—with many layers and different colors of vegetables and meat, enclosed in pastry—is quite celebrated in some circles. You see all the layers when you cut into it, so it makes for an impressive presentation.

9 large eggs

Salt and freshly ground black pepper

5 teaspoons unsalted butter, plus more for the cake pan

One 10-ounce package frozen whole-leaf spinach, thawed

4 teaspoons olive oil

2 cups (about 6 ounces) sliced white or cremini mushrooms

2 cloves garlic, minced

¼ cup heavy cream

One 16-ounce box frozen all-butter puff pastry, thawed overnight in the refrigerator

6 ounces domestic mozzarella cheese, grated

6 ounces sliced ham

One 12-ounce jar roasted red peppers, drained

In a medium bowl, beat 8 of the eggs with 4 teaspoons water and season with salt and pepper. Melt 1 teaspoon of the butter in a skillet over medium heat, add the eggs, and scramble them loosely, stirring with a wooden spoon until they're barely cooked through, about 2 minutes. (They will cook more in the oven.) Spoon the eggs onto a plate and let them cool.

Place the thawed spinach in a colander and use your hands to press out as much moisture as possible.

Heat 2 teaspoons of the butter and 2 teaspoons of the olive oil in a sauté pan over medium-high heat and sauté the sliced mushrooms until tender, 3 to 4 minutes, seasoning them lightly with salt and pepper. Transfer the mushrooms to a plate and set aside to cool.

{CONTINUED ON PAGE 67}

Heat the remaining 2 teaspoons butter and 2 teaspoons olive oil in the same sauté pan over medium-high heat and sauté the garlic for 30 seconds. Add the drained spinach and heat through. Add the heavy cream and cook, stirring to combine, for 1 minute. Remove from the heat and let cool. (You can prepare the spinach and mushrooms a day in advance and refrigerate them until ready to use.)

Generously butter a 9-inch round cake pan.

Unfold 1 pastry sheet onto a lightly floured work surface. Roll out the dough with a rolling pin to remove the creases, and then cut a round of dough the same size as the cake pan, using the bottom of the pan as a guide. Place the pastry on a baking sheet and chill it until you're ready to use it.

Roll out the second pastry sheet and cut out a slightly larger round (big enough to line the cake pan and have about 1 inch of dough hanging over the edges of the pan). If the dough becomes too warm and pliable, place it on a baking sheet and chill it for 15 minutes to make it easier to handle. Line the cake pan with this larger pastry round, gently easing the dough into the corners of the pan, leaving any excess dough to be trimmed later. Chill the dough in the cake pan in the freezer for 15 minutes.

To assemble the torta, remove the cake pan from the freezer and trim the overhanging dough to 1 inch. Spread half of the cooled eggs over the pastry in the pan. Spread half of the spinach over the egg, then half of the cheese, half of the mushrooms, half of the ham, and finally all of the peppers. Repeat in inverse order, layering the remaining ham, mushrooms, cheese, spinach, and ending with the remaining eggs. Fold the overhanging dough in over the filling. Make an egg wash by beating the remaining egg with 1 tablespoon water, and brush the edge of the pastry with egg wash. Place the refrigerated pastry round on top, and press down gently to join the edge of the round with the egg-washed edge of the pastry in the pan. Brush the top layer of pastry with egg wash. Use a knife to cut a small hole in the center of the top pastry layer, to allow steam to escape during baking; then score radiating lines away from the hole for decoration, if desired. With the decorative design, don't cut through the pastry; just scratch the surface. Chill the entire torta for 30 minutes to let the layers settle.

Position a rack in the lower third of the oven and heat the oven to 350 degrees.

Place the cake pan on a baking sheet and bake the torta for 1 to 1¼ hours, until golden brown on top. Let it cool for 10 minutes. Then cut it into wedges and serve.

BAKED EGGS
IN HAM CUPS

SERVES 4

This dish is simple to make but very attractive—the pastry chef in me loves that. Lining muffin tins with ham serves two purposes: It creates an edible container for the eggs, and it adds flavor. You can replace the mozzarella with another kind of cheese if you want a stronger cheese flavor; using fresh mozzarella makes this an authentic Italian dish, but its flavor is quite mild. When you're eating with guests, these are probably going to be knife-and-fork food—but when I was testing the recipe, I ate them with my hands, and that works too.

1 teaspoon unsalted butter, for the tins

Four $\frac{1}{16}$-inch-thick round ham slices (the largest you can find at the deli)

1 teaspoon pesto, homemade (page 139) or store-bought

8 large eggs

Eight $\frac{3}{4}$-inch cubes fresh mozzarella

4 cherry or grape tomatoes, halved

Salt and freshly ground black pepper

Heat the oven to 375 degrees.

Butter 4 compartments of a metal muffin tin. Fold each ham slice into quarters, insert the point end in a buttered muffin cup, and let it open—it will have a ruffled look. Place ¼ teaspoon pesto in the bottom of each ham cup, then carefully crack 2 eggs into each cup. (Sometimes I crack my eggs into a pitcher with a pour spout or into a small paper cup and pour them into the ham cup from there.) Tuck 2 mozzarella cubes and two cherry tomato halves into each cup on top of the eggs, and sprinkle with salt and pepper to taste. (Remember that the ham and pesto both lend saltiness to the dish.)

Bake for 15 to 20 minutes, until the egg white looks set but the yolk is still a bit runny. Remove the ham cups from the muffin tin and serve them in small bowls or lined up on a platter.

BACON AND EGG SALAD
SANDWICHES

MAKES 4 SANDWICHES

I've spent a good portion of my life searching for the perfect egg salad sandwich. I finally found one in New York City, at a deli on Seventh Avenue, somewhere in the low forties. Since then I've thought about ways I could make egg salad more of a breakfast food, so I could have it for every meal if I wanted. Bacon is just the ingredient to make it taste like a morning meal. I chop the bacon and fold it into a very mild egg salad—just like the one from the Seventh Avenue deli. Egg salad is incredibly easy—it's mostly about cooking the eggs perfectly. Julia Child taught me how to do that, and her technique works every time (see note). I'm not usually a white bread advocate, but for these sandwiches, it's the best choice.

8 hard-boiled eggs (see note, opposite), peeled

4 strips bacon, cooked and chopped

¾ cup mayonnaise

1 tablespoon Dijon mustard

Salt and freshly ground black pepper

8 slices white bread, crusts cut off

Roughly chop the hard-boiled eggs and put them in a medium bowl. Sprinkle in the bacon, add the mayonnaise and mustard, and stir with a fork. Taste, and season with salt and pepper. Spread the egg salad on each of 4 slices of bread, top each sandwich with another slice of bread, and cut corner to corner to make triangles. Serve immediately, or cover and chill for up to 3 hours before serving.

PERFECT HARD-BOILED EGGS

You'd think hard-boiling an egg would be easy—it's just an egg boiled in water. But many people overcook them, which causes the yolk to turn an unappetizing shade of khaki green and to become dry and crumbly. My friend Julia Child taught me how to make them correctly and they are exquisite every time, with sunny yellow yolks. And truly, it couldn't be easier: Place the eggs in a saucepan and cover them with cold water (the top surface of the water should be about 1 inch above the eggs). Lightly salt the water and bring it to a boil over high heat. As soon as the water is boiling, turn off the heat and let the pan sit for 10 minutes; that's enough to cook the eggs through without overcooking them. Then place the pan under cold running water and let it run until the water in the pan feels cool (this will help the shells separate more easily from the egg whites). Chill overnight before peeling, if possible. (Pencil an X on the ends of the eggs so you remember which ones are hard-boiled.) Peel the eggs under cold running water to remove any small pieces of shell. Submerged in a bowl of water and stored in the refrigerator, peeled hard-boiled eggs will keep for 2 more days.

FRIED
MATZOH

SERVES 4

I think this is one of those dishes that is delicious if you grew up with it and a bit of a mystery if you didn't. My Jewish mother made it, and most Jewish homes find it on the menu after Passover when there's leftover matzoh. It's a bit like French toast in that it's bread (matzoh, in this case) soaked with eggs and then pan-fried. Some people prefer this as a savory dish made with garlic or onions; some eat it only with strawberry jam or maple syrup. (I'm in the maple syrup camp.) This is a dish that kids can easily help make—the first step is breaking all the matzoh crackers into pieces.

4 sheets matzoh, preferably unsalted	5 grinds freshly ground black pepper
4 large eggs	1 teaspoon unsalted butter
¼ teaspoon salt	Maple syrup, for serving

Break the matzoh sheets into pieces about the size of Saltine crackers or smaller (irregular shapes are fine), and place them in a large bowl. Pour enough water over the pieces to cover them. Let soak for 10 minutes while you prepare the rest of the ingredients.

In a small bowl, beat together the eggs, 2 teaspoons water, the salt, and the pepper with a fork.

Place your hand, fingers stretched out wide, over the broken matzoh pieces and hold them in the bowl while you tip the bowl to let the excess water drain out; press on the matzoh to squeeze out some of the water. Add the egg mixture to the matzoh and use a fork to stir it in.

Heat the butter in a frying pan until it foams. Add the matzoh mixture and cook it on one side until golden brown, about 5 minutes. Then break up the mixture into 1-inch pieces, stir the pieces to cook them on the other side, and cook until they are done all the way through, 5 to 10 more minutes. Spoon onto plates and serve hot, with maple syrup.

SPINACH AND CHEDDAR
SOUFFLÉ

SERVES 4 TO 6

Making a soufflé might seem intimidating, but it shouldn't be. Just make sure to fold the egg whites in gently, and don't open the oven door while it's baking. I made this one recently and one of my three-year-olds, Ella, helped me, so how hard could it be? The spinach and cheese in this soufflé lend heft and structure, so it's less likely to collapse on you than a plain soufflé.

6 tablespoons unsalted butter, plus more for the soufflé dish

½ cup all-purpose flour

2 cups whole milk

1 teaspoon salt

¼ teaspoon freshly ground black pepper

2 pinches cayenne pepper

1½ teaspoons dry mustard

1 teaspoon dried thyme

2 cups shredded cheddar cheese

¼ cup grated Parmesan cheese

1 cup cooked spinach or thawed frozen spinach, well drained

6 large eggs, separated

Heat the oven to 375 degrees. Butter a 2-quart soufflé dish.

Melt the butter in a saucepan over medium heat, and then whisk in the flour. Cook the mixture until it bubbles a little and is straw colored, about 3 minutes. Drizzle in the milk, whisking constantly, and simmer until the mixture is thickened and smooth, about 2 minutes. Remove from the heat and add the salt, black pepper, cayenne pepper, mustard, thyme, cheddar, and Parmesan. Continue to whisk until the cheese melts. Whisk in the spinach and egg yolks, and let cool slightly.

Meanwhile, in a clean, dry bowl, whip the egg whites until soft peaks form. Barely fold a third of the egg whites into the cheese mixture, then barely fold in the second third, and then barely fold in the final third. Do not overmix. Pour the mixture into the soufflé dish and even out the top with a rubber spatula. Then run the tip of the spatula around the soufflé surface about 1 inch in from the edge of the dish to form a track. This will help it to rise straighter in the oven.

Bake on a baking sheet for 10 minutes. Then reduce the oven temperature to 300 degrees and continue baking for another 50 minutes. Remove the soufflé from the oven and serve immediately, in large spoonfuls.

POACHED EGGS AND PARMESAN

SERVES 4

Almost anything is better with a poached egg on top: pasta, salad, a sandwich, asparagus . . . the list goes on. Poaching the eggs for this dish is a fairly quick, time-sensitive, and hands-on process, so I don't usually make this for big groups. But you could try my friend Judy's trick. She pre-poaches the eggs, dumps them in cold water to stop the cooking, and keeps them there. Just before serving, she drops the eggs into simmering water for 1 minute to heat them up again. I like to use extra-virgin olive oil here, for the great flavor.

2 bunches medium asparagus (about 40 spears)

8 large eggs

1 teaspoon white vinegar

Salt

2 tablespoons extra-virgin olive oil

1 clove garlic, chopped

2 tablespoons unsalted butter

2 tablespoons fresh lemon juice

2 teaspoons finely chopped fresh parsley

Freshly ground black pepper

4 tablespoons coarsely grated Parmesan cheese

Cut off the bottoms of the asparagus spears. (To know how much to cut off, break one spear near the bottom and see where it snaps naturally. Using that as your guide, cut the bottoms off the rest of the spears in approximately the same place.)

Break the eggs into 8 individual containers, such as teacups, prep bowls, or paper cups. Prepare the poaching liquid for the eggs by bringing water, plus the vinegar and 4 pinches of salt, to a boil in a large, straight-walled, low-sided pan over medium-high heat.

Meanwhile, cook the asparagus: Bring salted water to a boil in a medium saucepan over medium-high heat. Add the asparagus and cook it until it is as tender as you like it (3 to 4 minutes for crisp-tender). Remove the cooked asparagus from the water with tongs, and set it aside while you make the sauce.

{CONTINUED ON PAGE 76}

To make the sauce, empty the water from the saucepan and dry it out. Add the olive oil and heat it over medium heat. Add the garlic and sauté for about 1 minute, enough to take the raw edge off but not to give it much color. Turn off the heat; then add the butter and swirl the pan. Add the lemon juice, parsley, and salt and pepper to taste, and swirl the pan again to mix the ingredients. Put the asparagus back in the pan, add 2 tablespoons of the Parmesan, and toss with the sauce to coat.

To poach the eggs, make sure the water is boiling, then slowly pour each cup of egg into the water. Let the eggs cook for about 2 minutes; then turn off the heat and remove the pan from the burner.

Meanwhile, divide the asparagus among 4 plates. Bring the plates of asparagus close to the pan of poached eggs, and place a folded clean kitchen towel next to the plates.

As quickly as possible after the eggs have cooked for 2 minutes, use a slotted spoon to fish the eggs, one at a time, out of the poaching liquid, blotting the bottom of the spoon on the towel to absorb excess moisture. Place 2 eggs on each mound of asparagus. Pour any remaining sauce over the eggs, and sprinkle the remaining 2 tablespoons Parmesan over the top. Serve immediately.

CODDLED EGGS

SERVES 4

Coddled eggs have the wonderful texture of a soft-boiled egg without the fuss—you don't have to deal with the shell once they are cooked. In England I bought myself an egg coddler, which is a little ceramic cup with a tightly fitting screw-on lid into which you can break eggs and sort of poach them. Don't worry—you don't need to go to England to get one for this recipe. If you don't have a proper egg coddler, you can certainly use ramekins to coddle eggs. I'm not sure where the idea came from, but we always serve the coddled eggs with toasted "soldiers," little strips of buttered toast, to dunk into the yolk. I've added some cheese to the traditional recipe to make it a little more interesting. If you're a blue cheese lover, this would be a good place for it.

1 tablespoon unsalted butter, for the ramekins

8 large eggs

Salt and freshly ground black pepper

4 tablespoons grated cheddar cheese

½ teaspoon chopped fresh parsley

Butter four 8-ounce ramekins. Crack 2 eggs into each ramekin, and season well with salt and pepper. Sprinkle the cheese and parsley over the tops of the eggs, and cover the ramekins tightly with foil.

Place the ramekins in a large shallow pan and fill it with enough water to reach halfway up the sides of the ramekins. Heat over high heat to bring the water to a boil; then place a lid on the pan and turn the heat down to medium-low. Simmer for 13 to 15 minutes, depending on how firm you like your yolks (the longer they cook, the firmer the yolks will be).

Using tongs, immediately remove the ramekins from the pan. Remove the foil, and serve the eggs in their ramekins.

CARAMELIZED-APPLE CRÊPES

PANCAKES,
WAFFLES, FRENCH TOAST
& OTHER SWEETS

BUTTERMILK PANCAKES

TENDER PANCAKES

CARAMELIZED-APPLE CRÊPES

BASIC WAFFLES

KATHY'S BACON WAFFLES

CHOCOLATE WAFFLES

ALMOND CIABATTA FRENCH TOAST

BAKED CINNAMON-APPLE FRENCH TOAST

PANETTONE FRENCH TOAST

PINEAPPLE NOODLE KUGEL

BLACKBERRY BREAD PUDDING

GOAT CHEESE CAKE WITH SLOW-COOKED QUINCE

STEEL-CUT OATS WITH SUGARED WALNUTS

CRANBERRY-ALMOND GRANOLA

GRANOLA-PEACH PARFAIT

BUTTERMILK
PANCAKES

MAKES TWELVE 3- TO 4-INCH PANCAKES

These are absolutely delicious, so it's worth the trip to the store to buy buttermilk, which adds a slightly tangy flavor and tenderness to the pancakes. They're so good they almost don't need syrup, although of course they are delicious with maple syrup, fresh berries, a fruit butter (page 196), or Lemon Cream (page 182) on top or with any of the variations on page 82. This is one of my favorite things to make with my kids—have your kids stir the batter. In fact, it's almost better to have kids stir the batter because you want it to be lumpy, and kids never overmix! You can double this recipe.

1 cup all-purpose flour	1 large egg
1 tablespoon sugar	1 cup buttermilk
¼ teaspoon salt	¼ cup whole milk
1 teaspoon baking powder	2 tablespoons unsalted butter, melted, plus more for cooking
½ teaspoon baking soda	

In a medium bowl, combine the flour, sugar, salt, baking powder, and baking soda. In a separate bowl, beat the egg with a fork and then mix in the buttermilk, milk, and melted butter. Pour the wet ingredients over the dry ingredients and combine with a wooden spoon, leaving plenty of lumps. Transfer the batter to a pitcher with a pour spout.

Heat a griddle or a large skillet over medium heat (after you've cooked a few pancakes, you may want to turn the heat down to medium-low so your pancakes don't brown too quickly). Melt 1 teaspoon butter on it (when the griddle starts to get dry as you're cooking, add more butter, 1 teaspoon at a time) and heat the butter until it foams. Pour about 3 tablespoons of the batter onto the griddle to make each pancake, leaving space in between for spreading. When the top of each pancake is done bubbling and no longer looks wet and the underside is lightly browned (about 3 minutes), flip the pancake and cook it on the other side until golden brown, about 2 minutes. Serve immediately, or keep warm on a plate in a 200-degree oven while you cook some more pancakes.

BUTTERMILK PANCAKE
VARIATIONS

CORNMEAL AND CHEDDAR

Replace ¼ cup of the flour with ¼ cup yellow cornmeal. Add ½ cup cheddar cheese, ⅛ teaspoon cayenne pepper, and ⅛ teaspoon dry mustard with the dry ingredients. Serve with hot Honey Butter (page 195).

CRANBERRY-ORANGE

Add ½ cup whole fresh cranberries (chopped in a food processor) and 1 teaspoon grated orange zest to the wet ingredients.

LEMON–POPPY SEED

Add 2 teaspoons grated lemon zest and 2 tablespoons poppy seeds to the wet ingredients.

TENDER
PANCAKES

MAKES ABOUT TWELVE 3- TO 4-INCH PANCAKES

There's a woman in Chicago named Ina Pickney whose license plate reads BKFST QN—and indeed, she's known around here as the breakfast queen. She makes pancakes called Heavenly Hots . . . and they are. The secret to a really tender pancake—which Ina shared with me—is to replace some of the flour with potato starch. The starch (also called potato flour) holds liquid differently and has a finer texture than wheat flour. (This is also a secret behind the original Krispy Kreme doughnut, and behind a long-lost brand of doughnut called Spud Nuts . . . shhhhh.) Try the pancakes with maple syrup, a fruit butter (page 196), Nana's Strawberry Preserves (page 193), or whipped cream and Strawberries in Syrup (page 185). You can double this recipe.

⅔ cup all-purpose flour

⅛ cup potato starch

1 tablespoon sugar

⅜ teaspoon salt

1½ tablespoons baking powder

1 large egg

1 cup whole milk

2 tablespoons canola oil

Unsalted butter, for cooking

In a medium bowl, combine the flour, potato starch, sugar, salt, and baking powder. In a separate bowl, beat the egg with a fork and then mix in the milk and oil. Pour the wet ingredients over the dry ingredients and combine with a wooden spoon, leaving plenty of lumps. Transfer the batter to a pitcher with a pour spout.

Heat a griddle or a large skillet over medium heat (you may want to turn it down to medium-low after you've cooked a few pancakes). Melt 1 teaspoon butter on it (add more butter, 1 teaspoon at a time, as you continue cooking and the griddle starts to get dry). Heat the butter until it foams. Pour 2 to 3 tablespoons of the batter onto the griddle to make each pancake, leaving space in between for spreading. When the top of each pancake has stopped bubbling and no longer looks wet and the underside is lightly browned (about 3 minutes), flip the pancake and cook it on the other side until golden brown, about 2 minutes. Serve immediately, or keep warm on a plate in a 200-degree oven.

CARAMELIZED-APPLE
CRÊPES

SERVES 4

I love apple pancakes. I grew up on the famous thick apple pancakes at Chicago's Walker Bros. pancake house. This is a thin, delicate apple pancake that I like just as well. The apples are embedded in an eggy crêpe batter, and just a dusting of powdered sugar is all they need.

2 large eggs

½ cup whole milk

¼ teaspoon salt

About 9 teaspoons sugar

½ cup all-purpose flour

About 4 teaspoons unsalted butter

2 Granny Smith or Honey Crisp apples, peeled, cored, and cut into very thin horizontal slices (so the slices have a hole in the center)

4 lemon wedges

Confectioners' sugar, for dusting

In a medium bowl, whisk together the eggs and the milk. Whisk in the salt, 1 teaspoon of the sugar, and flour. Set aside for 30 minutes.

In a nonstick 8- or 10-inch skillet, melt about 1 teaspoon of the butter over medium heat. Sprinkle in 2 teaspoons sugar and cook for about 1 minute to caramelize the sugar; it should be amber colored. Add 3 apple slices to the pan and cook them on one side for 1 to 2 minutes, until golden brown on the edges.

Pour or ladle one-fourth of the batter (about ¼ cup) over the apple slices. Lift and swirl the pan so the batter coats the bottom. Let cook until slightly browned on the underside, 1 to 2 minutes. Use a spatula or your fingers to flip the crêpe, and cook until the other side is slightly browned, about 1 minute. Don't worry if the batter pulls away from the apple a bit. Transfer the crêpe to a platter and keep warm in a 200-degree oven. Repeat this process, starting with the butter, to make three more crêpes.

Serve with a lemon wedge (for sprinkling lemon juice over the crêpes) and a dusting of confectioners' sugar.

BASIC WAFFLES

MAKES 3 TO 4 LARGE WAFFLES; SERVES 3 TO 4

You don't need any special ingredients for this basic recipe—so if it's early in the morning and you have a sudden craving for waffles, you can make them without having to run to the store for, say, buttermilk or cake flour. You can add ground spices like cinnamon and ginger to this straightforward batter or try one of the variations, but they're good plain too.

1¾ cups all-purpose flour

1 tablespoon baking powder

1 teaspoon salt

1 tablespoon sugar

2 large eggs

1½ cups whole milk

6 tablespoons unsalted butter, melted

Maple syrup, for serving

Heat a waffle iron.

In a medium bowl, stir together the flour, baking powder, salt, and sugar. In a separate bowl, whisk together the eggs, milk, and melted butter. Mix the dry ingredients into the wet ingredients all at once with a wooden spoon, until just combined. Don't overmix the batter; it should look lumpy.

For each waffle, pour ½ to 1 cup of the batter (or the amount recommended by the waffle-iron maker) onto the waffle iron; bake as directed by the manufacturer. Serve hot off the griddle, with maple syrup.

VARIATIONS

SPICED PECAN AND DRIED CHERRY

Add ¾ cup chopped pecans, ¾ cup chopped dried cherries, ½ teaspoon ground cinnamon, and ¼ teaspoon ground nutmeg to the dry ingredients.

PUMPKIN GINGERBREAD WAFFLES

Add 1 cup canned pumpkin puree to the wet ingredients and reduce the milk to 1¼ cups. Replace the sugar with molasses (add it to the wet ingredients) and add 1 teaspoon pumpkin pie spice to the dry ingredients.

KATHY'S
BACON WAFFLES

MAKES 4 TO 6 LARGE WAFFLES; SERVES 4 TO 6

This recipe idea came from my good friend Kathy Skutecki, who is a great cook. She points out that what we really like to do with our bacon is to dip it into maple syrup—so why not combine the bacon with waffles and give it the maple syrup bath it deserves, right from the start? I couldn't agree more.

2 cups all-purpose flour

1 tablespoon baking powder

¼ teaspoon baking soda

2 tablespoons sugar

2 large eggs

¾ cup buttermilk

¾ cup whole milk

4 tablespoons unsalted butter, melted

6 strips bacon, cooked and crumbled

Maple syrup, for serving

Heat a waffle iron.

In a medium bowl, stir together the flour, baking powder, baking soda, and sugar. In a separate bowl, whisk together the eggs, buttermilk, milk, and melted butter. Stir the crumbled bacon into the wet ingredients. Mix the dry ingredients into the wet ingredients all at once with a wooden spoon until just combined. Don't overmix the batter; it should be lumpy.

For each waffle, pour ¼ to 1 cup of the batter (or the amount recommended by the waffle-iron maker) onto the waffle iron; bake as directed by the manufacturer. Serve hot off the griddle, with maple syrup.

CHOCOLATE
WAFFLES

MAKES 3 TO 4 LARGE WAFFLES; SERVES 3 TO 4

Rich and chocolaty but not too sweet, these are definitely great for brunch, not just for dessert. The chocoholics in your life will thank you. You could serve these with vanilla yogurt, Strawberries in Syrup (page 185), Bananas Foster (page 183), or simply whipped cream, fresh raspberries, and a sprinkling of confectioners' sugar.

2 large egg yolks

1½ cups whole milk

2 teaspoons baking powder

1¼ cups all-purpose flour

¼ cup unsweetened cocoa powder

4 tablespoons unsalted butter, melted

2 large egg whites

2 tablespoons light brown sugar

Heat a waffle iron.

In a medium bowl, combine the egg yolks, milk, baking powder, flour, cocoa powder, and melted butter and mix until almost smooth. In the bowl of a mixer fitted with the whisk attachment, whip the egg whites until stiff peaks form; then add the brown sugar and continue whipping until stiff. Fold the whipped egg whites into the batter.

For each waffle, pour ½ to 1 cup of the batter (or the amount recommended by the waffle-iron maker) onto the waffle iron; bake as directed by the manufacturer.

ALMOND CIABATTA
FRENCH TOAST

MAKES 8 PIECES OF FRENCH TOAST; SERVES 4 TO 6

At Osteria di Tramonto, the Italian restaurant I own with my partners, we serve ciabatta, an Italian bread that has nice big, open holes inside. It's delicious fresh, but it really is not the same the next day . . . so, what to do with all the leftovers? We tried a bread pudding, but it was too firm for my taste. Then I tried making French toast with it—and it's divine! It's soft and tender from absorbing extra custard into all the spongy holes. Serve this with maple syrup or a dollop of ricotta cheese.

3 large eggs

2 pinches salt

3 tablespoons sugar

¼ teaspoon pure vanilla extract

¼ teaspoon almond extract

1¼ cups whole milk

¼ cup heavy cream

Eight 1-inch slices round ciabatta

Unsalted butter, for cooking

1 cup sliced almonds

Heat a griddle over medium-low heat.

In a medium bowl, whisk the eggs well. Whisk in the salt, sugar, vanilla, and almond extract. Gradually whisk in the milk and cream. Pour the mixture into a shallow baking dish. Working in batches if necessary, place the bread in the dish and let it soak for 3 minutes; then turn the slices over and soak on the other side.

Butter your griddle and let the butter bubble. Just before placing the soaked bread slices on the griddle, place almonds in a single layer (but fairly densely packed) on the griddle, forming an area the size and shape of a bread slice. Press one side of the bread into the almonds on the griddle, and cook until golden brown, about 4 minutes. Flip the bread to the other side and cook until speckled golden brown, 3 to 4 minutes. Serve hot.

BAKED CINNAMON-APPLE
FRENCH TOAST

SERVES 8

When relatives are staying with us and I want to serve French toast but I don't want to have to prepare it first thing in the morning, I use this recipe, which falls somewhere between French toast and bread pudding. I can prepare it the night before, so all I have to do when I wake up is wander down to the kitchen, heat the oven, and pop it in . . . and then steal another hour of sleep. I also love it because it uses up those questionable apples in my fruit drawer. (You have those too, don't you? Please say you do.)

6 medium apples (I use an assortment)

2 tablespoons unsalted butter, cut up into small cubes, plus more for the baking dish

½ cup packed light brown sugar

1½ teaspoons ground cinnamon

½ teaspoon ground nutmeg

8 slices Texas toast (thick presliced white bread)

8 large eggs

½ cup granulated sugar

3½ cups whole milk

1 tablespoon pure vanilla extract

Honey Butter (page 195)

Peel, core, and cut the apples into ¼-inch-thick slices. Heat the butter in a sauté pan over medium heat until it starts to foam. Add the apples and cook them until tender, about 10 minutes. Turn off the heat and stir in the brown sugar, cinnamon, and nutmeg. Set aside.

Lightly toast the bread. Cut the toast slices in half to make triangles. Butter a 9x13-inch baking dish, and arrange the bread in two rows, overlapping in the dish.

Beat the eggs in a medium bowl; then whisk in the sugar, milk, and vanilla to make a custard. Pour the custard over the bread triangles, and spoon the apples over the top. Cover, and refrigerate overnight.

The next day, heat the oven to 350 degrees.

Uncover the baking dish and bake for 50 to 60 minutes, until the custard is set and doesn't shimmy when you shake the pan. It will puff up and brown slightly. Remove from the oven and let it rest for 10 minutes before serving. Serve in squares or large spoonfuls, with honey butter.

PANETTONE
FRENCH TOAST

MAKES 8 SLICES; SERVES 4 TO 6

After Christmas I always find my kitchen stacked with loaves of panettone, the sweet, fruit-studded breakfast bread from Italy that's sold in puffy loaves and packaged in pretty red tins or boxes, sometimes with handles and beautifully detailed doily-like graphics. I think I'm drawn to the packaging as much as to the bread itself, and when I see it discounted in a post-holiday sale, I can't resist. I love it toasted, but when I go really crazy buying it, I need a higher-volume way to use it up. That's why I came up with this recipe, in which the golden bread does most of the work for you. That's my kind of ingredient! All you need to do is soak it in custard and grill it or bake it, and serve it with real maple syrup (no imitation syrup, please). If you don't have panettone, you can use challah or any rich egg bread. Stale bread is best, because it absorbs more of the custard than fresh bread will.

3 large eggs

1 pinch salt

¼ cup sugar

½ teaspoon pure vanilla extract

1 cup half-and-half

1 cup buttermilk

8 wedges panettone, each about 1½ inches thick at its widest end

1 to 2 teaspoons unsalted butter, for cooking

Maple syrup, for serving

Heat a griddle over medium-low heat.

In a medium bowl, whisk the eggs well. Whisk in the salt, sugar, and vanilla. Gradually whisk in the half-and-half and buttermilk. Pour the mixture into a shallow baking dish. Working in batches if necessary, place the bread in the dish and let it soak for 5 minutes; then turn the pieces over and soak on the other side for another 5 minutes.

Butter your griddle and let the butter bubble. Then place the soaked panettone slices on the griddle to brown, 3 to 4 minutes. When they're golden brown, flip them to the other side and cook for 3 to 4 minutes. Serve hot, with maple syrup.

PINEAPPLE
NOODLE KUGEL

SERVES 6 TO 8

Noodle kugel is one of those dishes that could go either way: to the savory side of the buffet or to the sweet side. It's a baked noodle casserole held together with sweet, creamy custard, often flavored with something like canned fruit. It's a popular dish to make for some Jewish holidays, and I think it's the perfect brunch dish anytime—for brunch I like anything that straddles the sweet-savory line. This pineapple version was inspired by my friend Al's sister, who would send one with him to Tru (a restaurant I co-own in Chicago) every year for one of the Jewish holidays. Covered, noodle kugel keeps for up to 4 days in the refrigerator without declining in flavor or texture, and it reheats well too.

8 ounces medium-wide egg noodles

Unsalted butter, for the baking dish

3 large eggs

8 ounces cottage cheese or farmer's cheese

4 ounces cream cheese

1 cup sour cream, plus more for serving (optional)

½ cup (1 stick) unsalted butter, melted

½ cup packed light brown sugar

1 pinch salt

½ teaspoon pure vanilla extract

1 cup canned or fresh cubed pineapple, drained and cut into smaller pieces

½ cup raisins

Bring a large pot of water to a boil, add the noodles, and boil until cooked through but not overcooked. Drain well and set aside in a large bowl.

Heat the oven to 350 degrees. Butter an 8-inch square baking dish.

In a blender, combine the eggs, cottage cheese, cream cheese, sour cream, melted butter, brown sugar, salt, and vanilla. Stir this into the drained noodles, along with the pineapple pieces and raisins. Pour into the prepared baking dish, and bake until the pudding is set and butter is bubbling around the edges, 30 to 40 minutes. Let cool for 10 minutes before serving.

Serve warm or at room temperature, cut into squares and topped with a dollop of sour cream, if desired.

BLACKBERRY
BREAD PUDDING

SERVES 6 TO 8

This dish could easily be a dessert, but it's also perfect for breakfast (as, I think, many desserts are). Blackberries can be tart, but this preparation mellows them. You can use frozen blackberries or replace them with another berry, such as strawberries, raspberries, blueberries, or even cranberries when they're in season.

½ large loaf brioche or challah (about 8 ounces)

2 cups half-and-half

2 cups heavy cream

1 pinch salt

6 large eggs

1 cup granulated sugar

1 teaspoon vanilla bean paste or pure vanilla extract

1 cup blackberries

Confectioners' sugar, for dusting

Heat the oven to 350 degrees.

Cut the crusts off the bread and cut the crustless bread into 1-inch cubes. (You should have about 3½ cups of bread cubes.) Scatter the bread cubes on a baking sheet and toast them in the oven until light golden brown, 10 to 15 minutes. Watch carefully to make sure they do not brown too much. Set aside to cool, leaving the oven on.

In a medium bowl, combine the half-and-half, cream, and salt. In a separate large mixing bowl, whisk the eggs, granulated sugar, and vanilla together. Whisking constantly, gradually add the cream mixture. Strain into a large bowl to remove any lumps. Add the bread cubes, toss gently, and let soak until they absorb the custard, 15 to 30 minutes, folding the mixture once after 5 minutes to ensure even soaking. Fold the blackberries in carefully, and pour into a deep 9x13-inch baking dish.

Place the dish in a large roasting pan and fill the roasting pan with enough hot water to reach about halfway up the sides of the baking dish, to create a hot water bath. Bake until the pudding is set and golden brown on top, 45 to 50 minutes. Remove the baking dish from the water bath and serve immediately, or let cool to serve warm or chilled. Serve by the large spoonful, dusted with confectioners' sugar.

GOAT CHEESE CAKE
WITH SLOW-COOKED QUINCE

SERVES 8 TO 10

This recipe takes the classic cheese and fruit combination and presents it in a unique way. When sweetened and baked into a cake, goat cheese gets close to the border between cheese course and dessert (a border where I like to spend a lot of time). Quince is a strange fruit. I fell in love with it when I lived in England in the 1990s and my ninety-one-year-old next-door neighbor, Mr. Peniston, grew them in his yard. They can't be eaten raw because they are too astringent, like a very unripe banana. But poaching them slowly in a sweetened liquid makes them tender, brings out their fragrant nature, and turns them a blushingly beautiful shade of pink. The cheesecake and cooked quince—a fantastic addition to a brunch buffet or a slightly sweet treat for a savory brunch—will keep for several days, covered, in the refrigerator. If you can't find quince, use apples instead and add ¼ cup grenadine to the cooking liquid to give the apples a rosy, quince-like glow.

FOR THE QUINCE
- 4 quince
- 2 cups sugar
- 2 cinnamon sticks

FOR THE CHEESECAKE
- Unsalted butter, for the pan
- 16 ounces fresh goat cheese
- 16 ounces cream cheese
- 1½ cups sugar
- 8 large eggs

Peel the quince and cut them in half. Remove the seed packet with a melon baller or a spoon, and then cut each half in half again, so you end up with quarters. Place the quince in a saucepan with 2 cups water, the sugar, and the cinnamon sticks, and cover with a piece of parchment paper. Simmer gently until the quince pieces are tender and pink, about 2 hours. Chill in their cooking liquid. (The quince can be poached up to 5 days in advance and refrigerated.)

Heat the oven to 325 degrees. Butter an 8-inch springform pan.

In a mixer with the paddle attachment on low speed, mix the goat cheese with the cream cheese until smooth and fully incorporated. Add the sugar and just mix it in. Add the eggs and continue mixing to blend them in. Pour the mixture into

{CONTINUED ON PAGE 99}

the prepared pan. Wrap the outside of the pan in foil and place it in a roasting pan. Fill the roasting pan with enough hot water to reach halfway up the sides of the springform pan.

Bake for about 90 minutes or until the cheesecake is puffed up and light golden brown around the edges. Remove the springform pan from the water and let the cheesecake cool for 2 hours. Then cover, and chill the cake in the pan for at least 4 hours or overnight.

To serve, remove the springform sides. Slice the cake and serve with the quince on the side.

═══ RETRIEVING BITS OF EGGSHELL ═══

Even after decades as a pastry chef, and countless eggs cracked, I still sometimes get flecks of eggshell in the bowl. When that happens, the easiest way to retrieve the errant shell pieces is with the eggshell itself—one of the intact halves you've cracked. It does a much better job than fingers or spoons of attracting bits of shell from the yolk or whatever other liquid they are swimming in.

STEEL-CUT OATS
WITH SUGARED WALNUTS

SERVES 4 TO 6

Steel-cut oats take a while to cook, but they are worth the wait. I get them started before everyone wakes up and turn the heat to low. By the time the family is ready for breakfast, so is the oatmeal. For everyday, top it with whatever is the favorite in your family, whether that's raisins and brown sugar or a pat of butter (my mom's preference). If you're entertaining, try it with a dollop of whipped cream and sugared walnuts—oatmeal has never been this decadent. This recipe makes more walnuts than you'll need, so you can keep some in an airtight container to snack on later or to sprinkle on ice cream.

1 cup steel-cut oats	Whipped cream, for serving
¼ teaspoon salt	Sugared Walnuts (opposite)

Bring 1 quart water to a boil in a 3-quart saucepan. Once it's boiling, stir in the oats and salt and turn the heat down to low. Let the oats simmer, stirring them occasionally, for at least 30 minutes and up to 45 minutes, until they are as tender as you want them to be.

Spoon the oatmeal into bowls, and top each one with a spoonful of whipped cream and a small handful of sugared walnuts.

SUGARED WALNUTS

MAKES ABOUT 2 CUPS

¾ cup sugar
   Grated zest of ¼ orange
1 pinch ground cinnamon
2 cups walnut halves

In a deep saucepan, combine the sugar, ⅓ cup water, the orange zest, and the cinnamon. Bring to a boil. Add the walnuts and simmer, stirring constantly. The glaze will be shiny and transparent at first. Then it will turn opaque and crystallized as the water evaporates. When the nuts are completely coated with sugar crystals, after 5 to 7 minutes, they are done. Spread them out on a baking sheet to cool. (Tip: To wash the saucepan, soak it in water overnight.)

CRANBERRY-ALMOND
GRANOLA

MAKES ABOUT 7 CUPS

My coauthor, Christie, came up with this recipe when she decided she wanted to stop buying processed breakfast cereals and make her own granola instead, from ingredients she could buy in bulk. She played around with dozens of combinations, and this is one of her favorites because it features cranberries, almonds, and coconut. The sea salt heightens the buttery taste, and the orange juice plays well against the cranberries. Make this in advance and serve it with milk or yogurt—and fresh berries, if desired.

½ cup honey

½ cup maple syrup

¼ cup orange juice

3 tablespoons unsalted butter

1 teaspoon almond extract

4 cups old-fashioned rolled oats

¾ cup unsweetened shredded coconut

1 cup chopped almonds

1 teaspoon sea salt

1 cup dried cranberries

Heat the oven to 325 degrees. Line a rimmed baking sheet with parchment paper.

Combine the honey, maple syrup, orange juice, butter, and almond extract in a saucepan. Bring to a boil over medium heat, being careful not to let the mixture boil over. Then reduce the heat and simmer for about 5 minutes, stirring often, until the mixture thickens slightly.

Mix the oats, coconut, almonds, and salt in a large bowl. Pour the hot honey mixture over the oat mixture, stir to coat thoroughly, and spread evenly on the baking sheet.

Bake for 14 minutes, stirring occasionally. Add the cranberries and bake for another 15 to 18 minutes, stirring occasionally, until golden brown. Remove the granola from the oven and let it cool completely. The granola keeps in an airtight container at room temperature for up to 2 weeks.

GRANOLA-PEACH
PARFAIT

SERVES 4

When peaches are in season, there's nothing better than pairing them with a little creaminess—in the form of yogurt, in this case. And granola adds the perfect amount of crunch. Use your favorite granola, or try the Cranberry-Almond Granola (opposite). When fresh peaches aren't in season, replace them with frozen organic ones.

2 ripe peaches, pitted and cut into chunks

1 cup strawberries, hulled and halved or quartered

2 tablespoons fresh lemon juice

2 tablespoons packed light brown sugar

2 cups granola

2 cups vanilla yogurt

Toss the peaches, strawberries, lemon juice, and brown sugar together in a medium bowl until the fruits are well coated. Chill, covered, for at least 1 hour and up to 8 hours.

In each of 4 glasses, layer ½ cup granola, then ½ cup yogurt, and then ½ cup macerated fruit. Serve immediately.

SPICED APPLE-RAISIN TURNOVERS

The
BAKERY

GINGER SCONES WITH PEACHES AND CREAM

BACON-SCALLION SCONES

SOFT GIANT PRETZELS

QUICK PEAR STREUSEL COFFEE CAKE

MOIST ORANGE-DATE MUFFINS

CHOCOLATE CHIP CRUMB CAKE MUFFINS

CRANBERRY ANGEL-FOOD MUFFINS

SPICED APPLE-RAISIN TURNOVERS

PEANUT BUTTER AND JELLY TURNOVERS

HAND-FORMED PEAR AND ALMOND TARTLETS

CINNAMON SUGAR DOUGHNUTS

GLAZED CRULLERS

GINGER SCONES
WITH PEACHES AND CREAM

MAKES 15 TO 18 SCONES

Crystallized ginger, which is sometimes called preserved or candied ginger, gives off a unique spiciness that complements sweet foods beautifully. It's especially delicious in these scones, which will definitely get you going in the morning. This recipe can be halved to make about 8 scones.

3¾ cups all-purpose flour

¼ teaspoon salt

¼ cup plus 2 teaspoons sugar

3 tablespoons baking powder

½ cup (1 stick) cold unsalted butter, cut into pieces

¼ cup chopped crystallized ginger

1¼ cups whole milk, plus more for brushing

¾ cup heavy cream

¼ cup sour cream

1 ripe fresh peach, cut into wedges, or ½ cup canned peaches, drained

1 tablespoon honey

Heat the oven to 375 degrees.

In a mixer fitted with the paddle attachment, or working by hand in a large bowl, combine the flour, salt, ¼ cup sugar, and baking powder on low speed. With the mixer running, add the cold butter and stir until the mixture is coarse and sandy. You should still be able to see small lumps of butter. Mix in the ginger. Add the milk and mix until almost combined. Do not overmix.

Turn the dough out onto a lightly floured surface. Knead the dough 10 times to bring it together. Using a lightly floured rolling pin, roll out the dough to about ¾ inch thick. Using a biscuit or cookie cutter, cut out 2½-inch rounds. Knead the scraps together just until combined, then roll out again, and continue cutting out rounds until all the dough is used. Brush the tops with milk, and sprinkle with 1 teaspoon sugar. Transfer to an ungreased baking sheet.

Bake until light golden brown, 15 to 20 minutes. Let cool on the baking sheet.

Meanwhile, whip together the heavy cream, sour cream, and remaining 1 teaspoon sugar until stiff peaks form.

To serve, split the scones in half. Spoon a dollop of whipped cream on each bottom half, add a peach wedge, drizzle with honey, and then prop the top on top.

BACON-SCALLION
SCONES

MAKES 12 SCONES

A few years ago I visited Elizabeth Falkner's San Francisco bakery and restaurant, Citizen Cake, where I spotted a bacon and leek scone on top of the pastry case. I didn't get to try it, but I've been thinking about it ever since. (That tells you a lot about me. Some women never forget a pair of shoes they saw in a shop window; I'm haunted by the memory of a scone.) Here's a version of that scone that I developed, using fresh scallions. This recipe can be halved.

3¾ cups all-purpose flour

3 tablespoons baking powder

½ cup grated Parmesan cheese, plus more for sprinkling

1 teaspoon paprika

1 teaspoon chopped fresh parsley

¼ teaspoon salt

¼ teaspoon freshly ground black pepper

½ cup (1 stick) cold unsalted butter, cut into ½-inch pieces

3 strips bacon, cooked and chopped

¾ cup sliced scallions (white and green parts)

1¼ cups whole milk, plus more for brushing

Heat the oven to 375 degrees.

In the bowl of an electric mixer fitted with the paddle attachment, or working by hand in a large bowl, combine the flour, baking powder, Parmesan, paprika, parsley, salt, and pepper at low speed. With the mixer running, add the cold butter and stir until the mixture is coarse and sandy. You should still be able to see small lumps of butter. Mix in the bacon and scallions. Add the milk and mix until almost combined. Do not overmix; there may still be some flour visible.

Turn the dough out onto a lightly floured surface. Knead the dough 10 times to bring it together and smooth it out. Then divide the dough in half and shape it into 2 balls.

Using a lightly floured rolling pin, roll the balls out into 1-inch thick disks. Use a knife to cut each disk into 6 triangles. Brush the tops with milk and sprinkle them liberally with Parmesan cheese. Transfer them to an ungreased baking sheet.

Bake until light golden brown, 15 to 20 minutes. Let cool on a baking sheet. Serve warm or at room temperature, within a few hours of baking.

SOFT
GIANT PRETZELS

MAKES 20 PRETZELS

My friend Karen gave me this recipe. It's a good one to make with kids, and leftovers pack well in lunchboxes. Boiling the dough before baking it gives the pretzels a nice chewy exterior, like a bagel. The baking soda in the water helps create a shiny surface; commercial bakeries use lye to achieve the same effect. Soft pretzels are an unexpected treat as part of a brunch bread basket, and they make a great accompaniment to soup. Serve these with Spicy Horseradish Mustard (page 199) for dipping, or with jam or a flavored cream cheese (page 198).

2 tablespoons plus 1⅓ cups warm water

1 package active dry yeast

⅓ cup packed light brown sugar

5 cups all-purpose flour, plus more for kneading

1 teaspoon sea salt or kosher salt, plus more for sprinkling

Unsalted butter, for the pans

½ cup baking soda

In the bowl of an electric mixer, combine the 2 tablespoons warm water with the yeast and stir by hand until the yeast is dissolved. Stir in the remaining 1⅓ cups warm water and the brown sugar. Fit the mixer with the dough hook and set the bowl on it. Mix on medium-low speed, gradually adding the flour and salt. Continue mixing until the dough forms a ball. Turn the dough out onto a lightly floured work surface and knead it until it is smooth, about 5 minutes.

Heat the oven to 475 degrees. Butter two baking sheets.

Combine 2 quarts water and the baking soda in a large saucepan, and bring to a boil.

Cut the dough into golf-ball-size pieces. Roll the balls into ½-inch-thick worms. Form each worm into a U shape; then cross the ends, twisting them at the middle. Fold the ends back down to meet the bottom of the U, and press to secure the dough. Drop the pretzels, a few at a time, into the boiling water and cook for 30 seconds. Then fish them out, using a slotted spoon or a spider, and place them on the prepared baking sheets. Sprinkle with sea salt. Repeat with the remaining dough.

When all the pretzels have been boiled and salted, bake them for about 8 minutes, until golden brown. Serve warm or at room temperature.

COFFEE CAKE

MAKES ONE 8-INCH SQUARE CAKE; SERVES 8

My grandma Elsie on my mother's side was a great baker in the Austro-Hungarian tradition. Strudels, poppy seed cakes, coffee cakes, and cookies always seemed to be in her kitchen when we visited. I found a great apple streusel coffee cake recipe in her card files when I became the keeper of those treasures. Here it is, revived, with my little twist of using pears instead of apples.

FOR THE CAKE

Unsalted butter, for the baking dish

1¼ cups all-purpose flour

2¼ teaspoons baking powder

½ cup sugar

½ teaspoon salt

½ teaspoon ground cinnamon

1 large egg

½ cup whole milk

4 tablespoons unsalted butter, melted

2 ripe pears (I like Bartlett), unpeeled, cored and chopped (1½ cups)

FOR THE STREUSEL TOPPING

½ cup sugar

¼ cup all-purpose flour

3 tablespoons cold unsalted butter, cut up

1 teaspoon ground cinnamon

Heat the oven to 400 degrees. Butter an 8-inch square baking dish.

To make the cake, combine the flour with the baking powder, sugar, salt, and cinnamon in a medium bowl. In a separate bowl, beat the egg and then mix in the milk and melted butter. Pour the wet ingredients into the dry ingredients, add the pears, and mix well. Pour this into the buttered baking dish.

To make the streusel, mix the sugar, flour, cold butter, and cinnamon in a bowl by pinching them together with your fingers until well combined. Sprinkle over the top of the batter.

Bake the cake for 30 to 35 minutes, until it is golden and dry on top. Cool in the pan, and then cut into squares. This cake keeps for up to 4 days, covered, at room temperature.

MOIST
ORANGE-DATE MUFFINS

MAKES 12 REGULAR MUFFINS OR 36 MINI MUFFINS

This recipe comes from my mom, Myrna. I found it in her recipe card file. It was originally a quick bread that she called Holiday Orange Bread. This recipe is typical of my mother: It's super-easy and requires only stirring, no creaming, and there's very little cleanup. You can make these full-size or mini, which are perfect if you're serving them with an assortment of other baked goodies. I think these are delicious with cream cheese; try the Autumn Spice Cream Cheese (page 198).

1 medium orange, washed

½ cup dates, pitted and chopped

½ cup pecans, coarsely chopped

2 tablespoons unsalted butter, melted

½ cup orange juice

1 cup sugar

1 large egg, beaten

2 cups sifted all-purpose flour

1 teaspoon baking soda

1 teaspoon baking powder

½ teaspoon salt

Heat the oven to 350 degrees. Line a regular muffin tin with 12 paper liners, or line mini muffin tins with 36 mini liners.

Cut the whole unpeeled orange into 8 sections, and chop them in a food processor. In a large bowl, combine the chopped orange with the dates, pecans, melted butter, orange juice, sugar, and egg. In a separate bowl, sift together the flour, baking soda, baking powder, and salt. Stir the dry ingredients into the wet ingredients until just combined. Spoon the batter into the lined muffin tins, filling the cups no more than three-quarters full.

Bake until the muffins are puffed up and firm in the center: 25 to 30 minutes for regular muffins, 15 to 20 minutes for minis. Serve warm or at room temperature.

CHOCOLATE CHIP
CRUMB CAKE MUFFINS

MAKES 24 REGULAR OR 12 EXTRA-LARGE MUFFINS

My husband is crazy for crumb cake, so this one is for him. If you're not accustomed to eating chocolate in the morning, try it. There's nothing better than starting the day with a little dose of it. The French do it all the time with their cups of cocoa and *pain au chocolat.* And if you ask me, the French really know how to live!

FOR THE TOPPING

- ¼ cup packed light brown sugar
- ⅓ cup all-purpose flour
- ¼ teaspoon ground cinnamon
- 3 tablespoons unsalted butter at room temperature, cut into pieces
- ⅓ cup mini chocolate chips

FOR THE MUFFINS

- 1½ cups all-purpose flour
- ½ cup unsweetened cocoa powder
- 1 teaspoon baking powder
- 1 teaspoon baking soda
- ½ teaspoon salt
- ½ cup (1 stick) butter
- 1 cup sugar
- 3 large eggs
- 1 teaspoon pure vanilla extract
- 1¼ cups sour cream

Heat the oven to 375 degrees. Line regular muffin tins with 24 paper liners or line extra-large muffin tins with 12 paper liners.

To make the topping, in an electric mixer fitted with the paddle attachment, combine the brown sugar, flour, and cinnamon and mix on low speed. Add the butter and mix on low speed until crumbly. The mixture will look sandy at first and then will bind into crumbs. This may take several minutes, so keep mixing until larger crumbs form. Add the chocolate chips and mix just until they are dispersed. (You can make this topping in advance and keep it in an airtight container in the refrigerator for up to a week.)

{*CONTINUED ON PAGE 114*}

To make the muffins, sift together the flour, cocoa powder, baking powder, baking soda, and salt in a bowl, and set aside. In the bowl of an electric mixer (no need to wash the bowl after making the topping) fitted with the whip attachment, beat the butter on medium speed until it is light and fluffy; then add the sugar and mix well. Mix in the eggs, one at a time, and then mix in the vanilla. Add a third of the dry ingredients and mix until barely combined. Then mix in a third of the sour cream. Repeat until all the dry ingredients and sour cream are added and mixed until just combined. Scoop the batter into the lined muffin tins, filling them about halfway.

Spoon the topping onto the tops of the muffins. Bake until the muffins are cooked through and the topping is golden brown: 20 to 25 minutes for regular muffins, 25 to 30 minutes for extra-large muffins. Serve warm or at room temperature.

CRANBERRY
ANGEL-FOOD MUFFINS

MAKES 12 MUFFINS

These muffins—which happen to be fat-free—have a wonderful light texture. It's worth the effort to sift the flour three times to get the right consistency. Tart cranberries punctuate the airy cake and make for a festive treat around the holidays—but I like these so much that I keep cranberries in my freezer all year so I can make them anytime.

1 cup plus 2 tablespoons cake flour

1½ cups sugar

1½ cups (8 to 10 large) egg whites

1¼ teaspoons cream of tartar

½ teaspoon salt

1 teaspoon pure vanilla extract

Grated zest of ½ orange

1 cup fresh or frozen cranberries, coarsely chopped in a food processor

Heat the oven to 375 degrees. Line a muffin pan with 12 paper liners.

Sift the flour with ½ cup of the sugar into a bowl. Sift the mixture two more times.

In the bowl of an electric mixer fitted with the whisk attachment, whip the egg whites on low speed until they are foamy and look like bubble bath, about 30 seconds. Add the cream of tartar and the salt, and continue whipping on medium speed for about 1 minute. Gradually add the remaining 1 cup sugar and whip until soft peaks form. With a rubber spatula, fold in the sifted flour mixture until almost incorporated. Then fold in the vanilla, orange zest, and chopped cranberries.

Fill the cupcake wrappers three-quarters full with batter. Bake for 15 to 20 minutes, until the muffins are puffed, cracked, and slightly browned on top. Remove from the oven, unmold, and let cool on a wire rack before serving.

SPICED APPLE-RAISIN
TURNOVERS

MAKES 8 TURNOVERS

Fragrant, spicy apple butter, which you can usually find at farm stands in the fall and at gourmet grocery stores year-round, is a quick and easy spiced apple filling for homemade turnovers. Kids can help make these—they will especially enjoy drizzling the icing at the end. Even with three kids and a busy schedule, I can get these into the oven for Saturday morning breakfast, no problem. Just remember to put the puff pastry in the refrigerator the night before to thaw.

½ cup apple butter

¼ cup applesauce

1 Granny Smith apple, peeled, cored, and chopped

¼ cup raisins

⅛ teaspoon ground nutmeg

One 16-ounce box frozen all-butter puff pastry, thawed overnight in the refrigerator

All-purpose flour, for rolling

1 large egg, beaten

½ cup confectioners' sugar

2 teaspoons milk

Heat the oven to 425 degrees.

In a small mixing bowl, combine the apple butter, applesauce, chopped apple, raisins, and nutmeg.

Lay the puff pastry sheets on a work surface and roll them out into 10-inch squares, using flour if the pastry sticks. Cut each sheet into four 5-inch squares. Use a pastry brush to apply beaten egg to all four edges of each square. Divide the apple filling evenly among the centers of the squares. Fold the squares in half diagonally over the filling, pressing the edges together. Use a fork to seal the edges completely by pressing the tines down to make a crimped pattern.

Arrange the turnover triangles on a baking sheet, and brush the surfaces with beaten egg. Bake until golden brown, about 25 minutes.

While the turnovers are baking, stir together the confectioners' sugar and milk in a small bowl to make a thick icing. (For a thicker consistency, add more confectioners' sugar.) Keep the icing covered until ready to use.

Remove the turnovers from the oven and transfer them to a wire rack to cool slightly. Drizzle icing over the surface of each turnover. Serve warm or at room temperature, the same day.

PEANUT BUTTER AND JELLY
TURNOVERS

MAKES 8 TURNOVERS

Peanut butter and jelly is one of my favorite classic combinations. But in the morning? Why not! I've been known to roll peanut butter and jelly into breakfast crêpes too. The duo certainly makes for an easy turnover filling. The only hard part is deciding whether your brood prefers creamy or chunky peanut butter. That debate is still raging at our house.

One 16-ounce box frozen all-butter puff pastry, thawed overnight in the refrigerator

All-purpose flour, for rolling

1 large egg, beaten

¾ cup peanut butter

¾ cup jelly or jam of your choice

½ cup confectioners' sugar or more if needed

2 teaspoons milk

Heat the oven to 425 degrees.

Lay the puff pastry sheets out on a work surface and roll them out into 10-inch squares, using flour if the pastry sticks. Cut each sheet into four 5-inch squares. Use a pastry brush to brush beaten egg along all four edges of each square. Place 1 heaping tablespoon peanut butter and 1 heaping tablespoon jam in the center of each puff pastry square and fold it in half diagonally, pressing the edges together to enclose the filling and working out any air. Use a fork to seal the edges completely by pressing the tines down to make a crimped pattern.

Arrange the pastry triangles on a baking sheet. Brush the surface of the turnovers with beaten egg. Bake until golden brown, about 25 minutes.

Meanwhile, stir together the confectioners' sugar and milk in a small bowl to make a thick icing. (For a thicker consistency, add more confectioners' sugar.) Keep the icing covered until ready to use.

Remove the turnovers from the oven and transfer them to a wire rack to cool slightly. Drizzle icing over the surface of each turnover. Serve warm or at room temperature, the same day.

HAND-FORMED
PEAR AND ALMOND TARTLETS

SERVES 4

These elegant tartlets are easy to prepare yet impressive enough for the fanciest brunch—or even for a dinner party. Of course, they'll work just fine for a casual brunch too. I like the texture sour cream adds to the tartlets, but some people prefer their fruit less adorned. So the decision about whether to include sour cream here is up to you—these fetching tartlets will taste great either way.

1 sheet frozen all-butter puff pastry, thawed overnight in the refrigerator

2 tablespoons almond paste or canned almond filling

4 teaspoons sour cream (optional)

¼ cup sugar

¼ teaspoon ground cinnamon

2 pears, peeled, cored, and cut into 8 wedges each

Heat the oven to 425 degrees. Line a baking sheet with parchment paper.

Use a sharp knife to cut the puff pastry sheet into 4 squares. Arrange them on the prepared baking sheet. Divide the almond paste into 4 equal balls. Flatten the balls and place one in the center of each of the puff pastry squares. If using the sour cream, drop 1 teaspoon per tartlet on top of that.

Combine the sugar and cinnamon and sprinkle about 1½ teaspoons cinnamon sugar over the sour cream (or the almond paste) on each of the squares. Place 4 pear wedges on top of the almond paste and sour cream in the center of each pastry square, two facing away from the center one way and two facing the other way. Trim the pointy end of the pear slices if necessary so they'll fit. Sprinkle each set of pears with another 1½ teaspoons of the cinnamon sugar.

Use your hands to gather the puff pastry up around the pear slices and press it onto the pears to bundle them snugly in the dough. (It won't look pretty at this point, but it will look beautiful once it bakes and puffs up.) Bake until golden brown on the edges, 25 to 30 minutes. Transfer them to a wire rack and let cool before serving.

CINNAMON SUGAR
DOUGHNUTS

MAKES FORTY 2-INCH SQUARE DOUGHNUTS

This is a restaurant-style doughnut: You do half the work a day in advance and then half the work on the day you want to serve them, so they'll be fresh. My mom made me cinnamon toast practically every morning when I was growing up, and my husband loves doughnuts, so these remind me of two of my favorite people.

½ cup whole milk

1⅓ cups plus 1 teaspoon sugar

1½ teaspoons active dry yeast

1 large egg

2½ cups all-purpose flour

½ teaspoon salt

⅛ teaspoon ground nutmeg

4 tablespoons unsalted butter, melted

Unsalted butter, for the parchment paper

Canola oil, for frying

1 teaspoon ground cinnamon

Warm the milk and the 1 teaspoon sugar in a small saucepan over low heat. Remove from the heat and add the yeast. Let sit for 5 minutes to proof.

In a small bowl, beat the egg with ¼ cup water. In a stand mixer fitted with the paddle attachment, mix the flour, ⅓ cup sugar, salt, and nutmeg. Add the yeast mixture, the egg mixture, and the butter. Remove the paddle, attach a dough hook, and mix until well blended and kneaded, about 15 minutes. Grease a large mixing bowl and place the dough in it. Cover with plastic wrap and chill it overnight.

Roll the dough out on a floured surface to about ¼ inch thick. Place it on a baking sheet, cover with plastic wrap, and chill for 30 minutes. Take the dough out of the refrigerator and cut it into 1½-inch squares. Butter a piece of parchment paper and line a baking sheet with it. Place the squares ½ inch apart on the parchment, and top them with another sheet of parchment, buttered side down. Place the baking sheet in a warm place for about 30 minutes for the dough to rise.

Heat 2 inches of the oil in a large pot to 375 degrees. Working in batches, fry the doughnuts for 1 to 2 minutes on each side, until golden. Drain on paper towels.

In a large bowl, combine the remaining 1 cup sugar and the cinnamon. Toss the warm doughnuts in the cinnamon sugar. Serve these the same day you make them.

GLAZED
CRULLERS

MAKES 12 CRULLERS

What most people consider a cruller is a doughnut leavened with yeast or baking powder that's shaped into a long twist, deep-fried, and sprinkled with sugar or glazed with a thin icing. But this recipe is for a traditional French cruller, which is considerably lighter and airier. It's made from pâte à choux pastry and is basically hollow. I just love anything made from pâte à choux, the base of cream puffs and éclairs. What could be better than fried dough glazed with icing?

½ cup (1 stick) unsalted butter

½ teaspoon salt

1¼ teaspoons granulated sugar

1 cup all-purpose flour

3 to 4 large eggs

2 cups confectioners' sugar

¼ cup whole milk

Canola oil, for frying

Combine 1 cup water with the butter, salt, and granulated sugar in a large saucepan and bring to a boil over medium-high heat. Immediately take the pan off the heat. Add all the flour at once and stir hard with a wooden spoon until thoroughly incorporated, 30 to 60 seconds. Return the pan to medium heat and cook, stirring, for 2 minutes to allow some of the moisture to evaporate.

Scrape the mixture into the bowl of a mixer fitted with the paddle attachment (or use a hand mixer), and mix at medium speed. With the mixer running, add 3 of the eggs, one at a time, stopping after each addition to scrape the sides of the bowl. Mix until the dough is smooth and glossy. The dough should be thick, but it should fall slowly from the beaters when you lift them out of the bowl. If the dough is still clinging to the beaters, add 1 more egg and mix until completely incorporated.

Line a baking sheet with parchment paper. Using a pastry bag fitted with a star tip, pipe the dough in 2½-inch rings onto the parchment. Pipe rows of rings and then freeze them for 30 minutes to make them easier to pick up.

While the crullers are freezing, make the glaze by stirring the confectioners' sugar and milk together in a small bowl until smooth.

Heat 2 inches of oil in a deep fryer to 325 degrees. Working in batches, slip the dough rings into the hot oil. After 2 to 3 minutes, turn them over to brown evenly. Drain on paper towels, dip the top of each cruller in glaze, and let cool.

HERBED MINI POPOVERS

Brunch
BITES

GOUGÈRES

HERBED **MINI POPOVERS**

MINI **POTATO PANCAKES** WITH SMOKED SALMON

PANINI **FINGER SANDWICHES**

CRUNCHY **ZUCCHINI ROUNDS** WITH ROASTED
TOMATOES AND GOAT CHEESE

MOZZARELLA AND WHITE **NECTARINE
SKEWERS WITH PESTO**

FRIED QUAIL EGGS ON EGGNOG FRENCH TOAST

POTSTICKERS WITH SOY DIPPING SAUCE

GOUGÈRES

MAKES 50 TO 75 GOUGÈRES

I could eat an entire batch of gougères (pronounced goo-ZHAIRZ) myself. They're warm, buttery, eggy, tender, and light, and perfect on a brunch table or with cocktails, as a snack to start stimulating your guests' appetites. Serve them in a basket lined with a cloth napkin.

1 cup whole milk

6 tablespoons unsalted butter

1 cup all-purpose flour

1 teaspoon salt

3 to 4 grinds freshly ground black pepper

4 large eggs

1 cup grated Swiss-style cheese, such as Gruyère or Fontina

1 teaspoon Dijon mustard

1 teaspoon dry mustard

¼ teaspoon cayenne pepper

1 clove garlic, chopped

½ teaspoon chopped fresh parsley

2 tablespoons grated Parmesan cheese

Position a rack in the top third of the oven, and heat the oven to 425 degrees. Grease two baking sheets or line them with parchment paper.

Heat the milk and 4 tablespoons butter in a medium saucepan over medium-high heat, stirring occasionally to keep the bottom from burning. When the mixture is simmering and the butter has melted, remove from the heat and add the flour, salt, and black pepper all at once. Stir well with a wooden spoon to combine. Return the pan to medium heat and stir hard for 1 to 2 minutes, until the mixture thickens further and becomes stiff. Turn off the heat and stir a bit more to cool the mixture slightly.

Add the eggs, one at a time, beating well to incorporate each egg before adding the next. (You can beat in the eggs in the saucepan with a wooden spoon, or transfer the mixture to a mixer and use the paddle attachment to incorporate the eggs.) Then stir in the cheese, Dijon mustard, dry mustard, and cayenne and mix until smooth. Transfer the mixture to a pastry bag with a large plain tip. The mixture will still be warm.

Pipe the mixture onto the prepared baking sheets in mounds about the size of chocolate kisses, about 1 inch in diameter, leaving a couple of inches between mounds. Smooth out any points on the tops with a fingertip dipped in flour. (The dough can be prepared up to this point, covered in plastic wrap, and refrigerated for up to 8 hours or frozen for up to 1 week. Thaw at room temperature before baking.)

Bake the gougères for 10 minutes. Then reduce the oven temperature to 375 degrees and continue baking until golden brown, 8 to 10 minutes more. Let them cool slightly on the baking sheets.

While the gougères are cooling, melt the remaining 2 tablespoons butter in a small sauté pan over medium-low heat. Add the garlic and cook for 30 seconds. Add the parsley, swirl the pan, and then remove it from the heat. Drizzle the garlic-parsley butter over the gougères, and then sprinkle with the Parmesan. Serve immediately, while they're still warm.

HERBED
MINI POPOVERS

MAKES 12 TO 24 MINI POPOVERS, DEPENDING ON PAN SIZE

When popovers arrive in a bread basket at a restaurant, don't you get excited? I do! They're light, crusty, eggy, cavernous, and delicious all at once. Popover dough is related to pâte à choux, the pastry used for cream puffs, éclairs, and gougères (page 126), and is leavened only by the steam created from heating the liquids (milk and eggs) in the dough. No baking powder or baking soda here. These come out best if you have a proper mini popover pan, but you can also use a mini muffin tin; they just won't be quite as thin and tall. The key to good popovers is temperature: Follow the instructions and use a hot pan, and make sure the oven stays hot (no peeking during the first 20 minutes of baking). Serve these with Asparagus, Black Truffle, and Gouda Quiche (page 54) or a Caviar and Crème Fraîche Omelet (page 43). Try them with some kind of spread, such as the Lemon Butter on page 196.

2 large eggs

1 cup whole milk

1 cup sifted all-purpose flour

½ teaspoon salt

1 tablespoon chopped fresh tarragon or other savory herb

3 tablespoons unsalted butter

Fill a medium saucepan with an inch of water and bring it to a simmer. In a medium heatproof bowl, whisk together the eggs and the milk. Place the bowl over the simmering water and whisk the egg mixture constantly to warm it up to room temperature. Remove the bowl from the heat and whisk in the flour, salt, and tarragon just until combined; the batter should be lumpy. Transfer the batter to a pitcher with a pour spout and let it sit, covered with plastic wrap for about 1 hour at room temperature to tenderize the flour. (You can mix the batter a day ahead and keep it, covered, in the refrigerator.)

Heat the oven to 450 degrees. When the oven is hot, place a mini popover pan or mini muffin tin in the oven and let it heat for about 10 minutes.

{CONTINUED ON PAGE 130}

Melt the butter in a small saucepan over medium-low heat, and have a pastry brush ready. Remove the hot popover pan from the oven and quickly brush the cups well with the melted butter. Then quickly pour the batter into the cups, filling them about halfway. Bake for 15 minutes (this is when they'll puff up). Then turn the oven temperature down to 375 degrees and bake for another 5 to 10 minutes, until the popovers have risen up high over the edge of the cups and are nicely browned, but not too dark brown. (Don't open the oven door at all during the first 20 minutes of baking; the popovers are being leavened by steam and could easily deflate. Check after 20 minutes to make sure they aren't getting too dark.) Serve immediately.

MINI POTATO PANCAKES
WITH SMOKED SALMON

MAKES 36 PIECES

Bite-sized potato pancakes are fun and satisfying little treats. Smoked salmon has an intense flavor and makes for a great hors d'oeuvre any time of the day. Kids love these pancakes, and if they don't like smoked salmon you can leave it off the kids' tray. When I made these for a brunch for my friend Neil Steinberg and his family, they disappeared fast. I didn't even get one!

4 large russet potatoes, washed and quartered (do not peel)

1½ medium yellow onions, peeled and quartered

2 large eggs

1 teaspoon salt

¼ teaspoon freshly ground black pepper

1 cup all-purpose flour

Canola oil, for frying

1 cup sour cream

4 ounces sliced smoked salmon or lox, cut into 1-inch pieces

Chopped fresh chives, for garnish (optional)

Working quickly (before the potatoes discolor), shred the potatoes and onions in a food processor. Replace the shredding blade with the regular pureeing blade and return a third of the potato-onion mixture to the processor. Puree it well, then toss the puree with the shredded potatoes and onions. If the mixture is liquidy, let it drain through a colander for 3 minutes, then return it to the bowl.

In a small bowl, beat the eggs with the salt and pepper. Pour the beaten eggs over the potato mixture and toss with your hands. Sprinkle the flour over the top and toss the mixture again with your hands, mixing it gently to incorporate the flour.

Pour a little less than ¼ inch of oil into a nonstick frying pan, and heat over medium heat for about 1 minute. Working in batches, form 1-inch balls of the potato mixture, place them in the hot oil, and then flatten them slightly with the back of a spoon. Cook until well browned on one side, about 5 minutes; then flip them and repeat on the other side, about 5 minutes. Drain on paper towels and let cool. The pancakes can be made up to 2 hours ahead.

Serve the pancakes at room temperature topped with a small spoonful of sour cream and a piece of smoked salmon. Garnish with a sprinkling of chives, if desired.

PANINI
FINGER SANDWICHES

MAKES 4 TO 5 FINGERS

Last Christmas I bought my brother-in-law, Vinnie, a panini grill so he could make grilled Italian-style sandwiches. While I was waiting in line to pay for it, I felt a twinge of jealousy, which turned into serious envy, which blossomed into full-on covetousness. I turned around and got a second grill—for myself. Then I discovered a great universal truth: Everything is better when it's cooked on a panini grill. It grills both sides at the same time while pressing the bread slightly, resulting in warm, crispy deliciousness. Think of this recipe as a mere starting point—you can play with all kinds of combinations (I've included a few variations to help you). When I make these for a brunch, I like to offer several different kinds. Serve a panini finger with a demitasse of soup for a mini soup-and-sandwich combo.

2 teaspoons unsalted butter, at room temperature

2 slices round Tuscan or other rustic, country white bread

½ medium tomato, sliced

3 to 4 ounces fresh mozzarella, sliced

3 basil leaves

Heat a panini grill to medium.

Butter one side of 1 slice of bread and place it, butter side down, on a work surface. Layer the tomato, mozzarella, and basil on the bread and top with the second slice of bread. Butter the top of that slice. Place the sandwich in the grill and toast until golden brown, 4 to 6 minutes. Once it's grilled, let the sandwich rest for 1 minute; then cut it into 1-inch strips, and serve.

PANINI
VARIATIONS

Here are a few combinations I like for panini.
Use these in place of the tomato, basil, and mozzarella,
or experiment with other fillings of your choice.

| ROASTED RED OR YELLOW BELL PEPPER STRIPS AND MUENSTER CHEESE | SLICED PROSCIUTTO, ARUGULA, AND PROVOLONE CHEESE | HAM, BLANCHED ASPARAGUS SPEARS, AND SMOKED CHEDDAR CHEESE | COOKED BACON, SAUTÉED MUSHROOMS, AND MONTEREY JACK CHEESE |

CRUNCHY ZUCCHINI ROUNDS
WITH ROASTED TOMATOES AND GOAT CHEESE

SERVES 8 TO 10

These are easy to throw together once you have the tomatoes roasted, and that part can be done up to 4 days ahead of time. I like having these tomatoes on hand in any case—to toss into pasta, serve with cheese, or slap onto a panini. Here they're a great match for the creamy, mild goat cheese. You could substitute oil-packed sundried tomatoes in a pinch. I like to use extra-virgin olive oil for this, because it's just drizzled on top and gives such a nice flavor.

2 medium zucchini

Salt and freshly ground black pepper

Oven-Roasted Tomatoes (page 136)

3 ounces fresh goat cheese

2 tablespoons chopped fresh chives

2 tablespoons extra-virgin olive oil

Slice the zucchini into ¼-inch-thick rounds and lay them out on a platter. You should have about 24 slices. Sprinkle them with a little salt and pepper. Place 1 piece of roasted tomato on each zucchini slice. Pinch a bit of goat cheese on top of each tomato piece. Sprinkle with the chopped chives, drizzle with the olive oil, and serve.

OVEN-ROASTED TOMATOES

MAKES 24 PIECES

I use *herbes de Provence* here—a mixture of dried herbs commonly used in the south of France that often contains basil, fennel seed, lavender, marjoram, rosemary, sage, summer savory, and thyme. You can substitute any almost any dried or fresh herbs that you have on hand.

- 6 plum tomatoes
- ¼ cup olive oil
- 2 teaspoons *herbes de Provence*
- ½ teaspoon kosher salt
- ¼ teaspoon freshly ground black pepper

Heat the oven to 325 degrees.

Cut the tomatoes into quarters lengthwise. Lay them on a baking sheet, drizzle with the olive oil, and sprinkle with the *herbes de Provence,* salt, and pepper. Roast in the oven for about 2 hours, until the tomatoes are dried and wrinkled and their edges look lightly toasted. Check occasionally to make sure the edges aren't getting too brown. If they are, turn the oven temperature down to 300 degrees.

Use immediately, or store in an airtight container and refrigerate for up to 4 days. Let the tomatoes come to room temperature before serving.

MOZZARELLA AND WHITE
NECTARINE SKEWERS WITH PESTO

SERVES 8

White nectarines are delicious—more floral smelling and tasting than regular nectarines or peaches (which would also work here if you can't find white nectarines). Stone fruits with fresh mozzarella and pesto make a wonderful sweet and savory combination that your guests will remember. When you're buying nectarines or peaches, opt for those that have a strong fragrance when you sniff them, and check the seam along one side: It should be full and almost undetectable. A nectarine or peach that was picked too early will have a deep indentation at the seam. Once nectarines are ripe enough that they give under the pressure of my thumb, I like to refrigerate them. But for the most flavor, I always bring them to room temperature before eating them. Not everyone (I won't name names here—you know who you are) in my household agrees with this, but I like to remind them who has the James Beard Award in our home. I keep it in the kitchen to back me up on matters like these.

1 pound fresh mozzarella

3 medium-size ripe white nectarines or peaches

½ cup pesto, homemade (page 139) or store-bought

Olive oil, if needed

Cut the mozzarella into ¾-inch cubes. Cut each nectarine into 6 wedges, and then cut each wedge in half (for a total of 36 pieces, meaning you'll have a few extra to snack on). Use toothpicks to skewer alternating cubes of mozzarella and nectarine pieces, using 2 cubes and 2 nectarine pieces for each toothpick, and place them on a serving platter. Drizzle them with the pesto, and serve. (If the pesto is too thick to drizzle, thin it with a little olive oil.)

PESTO

MAKES ABOUT 1½ CUPS

- 2 cups packed basil leaves
- 2 large cloves garlic
- ½ cup olive oil
- 2 tablespoons unsalted butter, melted
- ½ cup pine nuts
- ½ teaspoon salt
- ⅛ teaspoon freshly ground black pepper
- ¾ cup grated Parmesan cheese

Combine the basil and garlic in a food processor and pulse to chop. Add the olive oil, butter, pine nuts, salt, pepper, and Parmesan and process until smooth and thick. Use immediately or freeze for a later use, such as tossing with pasta or spreading on Panini Finger Sandwiches (page 132).

FRIED QUAIL EGGS
ON EGGNOG FRENCH TOAST

MAKES 12 PIECES

This is a great recipe for using up leftover eggnog during the holiday season. It glorifies and elevates the fried egg sandwich, one of my (and my husband's) favorite late-night quick dinners. (Aren't we fancy?) I usually purchase quail eggs at a gourmet grocery store—they are definitely becoming more readily available and come in miniature divided cartons. Though it may seem fussy to pre-break the eggs into individual containers (use shot glasses, teacups, sake cups, or paper cups), it's very helpful because quail egg shells don't break easily. You have to pry them open a bit, and it's better to do that work before you start cooking.

2 cups eggnog

1 baguette, cut into twelve ½-inch-thick slices

12 quail eggs

1 link mild Italian sausage or 3 links breakfast sausage, casing removed

Butter, for cooking

Salt and freshly ground black pepper

1 teaspoon chopped fresh parsley (optional)

Pour the eggnog into a shallow pan and lay the bread slices in the eggnog to soak. After 5 minutes, flip the slices over to soak the other side. Meanwhile, break the quail eggs into individual little cups or glasses.

Heat a griddle or a large nonstick frying pan over medium-high heat. Break the sausage into 12 small nuggets, flatten them a little into mini patties, and cook them on both sides until lightly browned and cooked through, about 2 minutes. Remove them from the pan and set them aside. (These will sit on top of the French toast.)

To brown the French toast, melt about 1 teaspoon butter on the griddle and let it bubble (or you can use the fat from the sausage for extra flavor). Place the soaked bread slices on the griddle and brown them on both sides, 2 to 3 minutes per side. Spread them out on a platter and top each one with a nugget of cooked sausage.

Heat a little more butter on the griddle until it bubbles, and pour in the quail eggs, leaving space between them. Season the eggs with salt and pepper, and cook sunny side up for 1 to 2 minutes. Place a fried egg on top of each piece of sausage and serve, sprinkled with parsley, if you like.

POTSTICKERS
WITH SOY DIPPING SAUCE

MAKES ABOUT 4 DOZEN POTSTICKERS

This recipe comes from my good friend and occasional cooking partner Kathy Skutecki. I wanted to include a potsticker recipe here because they are a traditional Asian brunch food—and because kids love them. Even my picky eaters! As I was working on the book, Kathy was finishing teaching a class on how to make them. I knew hers would be as good as mine—probably better. Any extra filling can be tightly wrapped in plastic wrap and frozen for up to 1 month; or you can form it into small meatballs and poach them in chicken broth for a nice addition to a soup.

8 ounces ground pork, chicken, or turkey

8 ounces napa cabbage, finely chopped

2 teaspoons grated fresh ginger

½ cup chopped salted cashews

2 scallions (white and green parts), finely chopped

2 tablespoons soy sauce

1½ teaspoons Chinese rice wine or dry sherry

1 teaspoon toasted sesame oil

½ teaspoon salt

1 pinch ground white pepper

2 10.5-ounce packages frozen round dumpling or gyoza wrappers, defrosted overnight in the refrigerator

Canola oil, for frying

Soy Dipping Sauce (page 143)

To make the filling combine the pork, cabbage, ginger, cashews, scallions, soy sauce, rice wine, sesame oil, salt, and white pepper in a large bowl. Set it aside. (The filling can be made 1 day ahead and kept, covered, in the refrigerator.)

Line two baking sheets with parchment paper or aluminum foil. Spread out the dumpling wrappers on the baking sheets. Use a spoon to place 1 heaping tablespoon of filling in the center of each wrapper. Use your fingertip to wet the entire outer edge of the wrapper with water. Fold the wrapper to form a half-moon shape, pinching to seal it in the center only.

While holding a dumpling with the curved side up, use your index finger and thumb to fold one edge of the dumpling into pleats, pressing each pleat against

{CONTINUED ON PAGE 142}

the flat edge of the dough to seal it as you go. To do this, start at the center of the dumpling and work your way to the end, making three to four pleats. Then work from the center to the other end, creating another three to four pleats. While you do this, firmly press the pleated side of the wrapper against the flat side to be sure the dumpling is completely sealed. Taking time to pleat the dumpling wrapper gives it a nice rounded shape and allows it to sit upright on a serving platter. If there's too much filling, remove the extra to prevent leakage during cooking. (You can make the dumplings up to this point and freeze them for up to 2 months. Freeze them on a baking sheet until they are solid; then transfer them to a resealable plastic bag and freeze them for up to 2 months. Defrost before proceeding with the recipe.)

When you are ready to cook the dumplings, heat a few tablespoons of oil in a large deep skillet over medium heat until it is very hot but not smoking.

Place the dumplings in the skillet with the pleated side up, and press down gently so they stand up. Fry the dumplings for about 4 minutes, until they firm up slightly and their bottoms are golden brown. Pour ¼ cup cold water into the pan (careful, it will spatter) and quickly cover with a tight-fitting lid. Steam for about 6 minutes, or until the filling is cooked through.

Remove the lid and continue to cook for a few more minutes to evaporate any remaining liquid and re-crisp the bottoms.

Serve hot, with the dipping sauce on the side.

SOY DIPPING SAUCE

MAKES ABOUT ⅔ CUP

½ cup soy sauce

1 tablespoon Chinese black vinegar

1 tablespoon toasted sesame oil

1 pinch ground white pepper

Chinese hot pepper sauce or paste, to taste

Combine the soy sauce, vinegar, sesame oil, white pepper, and hot sauce in a small bowl. (The dipping sauce keeps, covered, in the refrigerator for 4 days.)

POACHED SALMON WITH CUCUMBER YOGURT

More
SAVORIES
& SOME SIDES

CHEESE AND **TOMATO GALETTE**

CARAMELIZED **ONION TARTS**

POACHED SALMON WITH CUCUMBER YOGURT

CORN AND **PARMESAN FRITTERS**

GOOEY **CAMEMBERT IN A BOX** WITH
CRANBERRY–BLACK PEPPER COMPOTE

GOAT CHEESE AND CHIVE **HASH BROWNS**

HOMEMADE PORK AND MAPLE **SAUSAGE PATTIES**

CHEESY CHEDDAR **GRITS**

GRILLED **PARMESAN** AND BLACK
PEPPER **POLENTA**

HAM AND VEGETABLE **SCRAPPLE**

CHEESE AND TOMATO
GALETTE

SERVES 6 TO 8

This is similar to a quiche but lower and flatter, so I make it in a flan mold or a shallow fluted ceramic quiche pan. If you use a standard pie pan, you may need to increase the baking time. You may have leftover dough from the tender crust recipe—when I do, I ball it up and use it to make a mini free-form galette for my kids. You can use any blanched vegetables you have for this (it's great with asparagus), but I really like the acidity of the tomatoes with the mellow custard. This is best served the day you make it because the crust gets a little soggy on day two; but it will keep in the refrigerator, covered, for up to 3 days.

FOR THE CRUST

- 2½ cups cake flour, plus more for rolling
- 1 teaspoon sugar
- ½ teaspoon salt
- ½ cup (1 stick) cold unsalted butter, cut into pieces
- 2 large egg yolks
- 3 tablespoons sour cream

FOR THE FILLING

- 3 large eggs
- ½ cup heavy cream
- 1½ cups whole milk
- 1½ cups shredded Swiss cheese
- 1½ cups shredded extra-sharp cheddar cheese
- ¼ cup grated Parmesan cheese
- 4 slices bacon, cooked and chopped (optional)
- 1 tablespoon chopped fresh parsley
- 1 tablespoon chopped fresh chives or ¼ cup chopped scallions (white and green parts)
- 3 gratings whole nutmeg or 3 pinches ground nutmeg
- 6 drops Tabasco or other hot sauce
- 2 medium tomatoes, sliced ¼ inch thick

{CONTINUED ON PAGE 148}

To make the crust, in the bowl of an electric mixer fitted with the paddle attachment, combine the flour, sugar, and salt on low speed. Add the cold butter and mix on low speed until it looks pebbly. In a small bowl, combine the yolks and sour cream. Pour this into the mixer bowl and mix on low speed until the dough almost comes together and no flour remains at the bottom of the bowl. Turn the dough out onto a work surface and form it into a disk. Wrap it in plastic wrap and refrigerate it for at least 1 hour.

On a floured work surface, roll the dough out ⅛ inch thick. Line a 4-cup-capacity ceramic flan pan or quiche dish with the dough, trimming off any excess. Chill the dough in the pan while you make the filling.

Heat the oven to 375 degrees.

To make the filling, whisk together the eggs, cream, and milk in a bowl until smooth. Stir in the three types of cheese, the bacon (if using), and the parsley, chives, nutmeg, and Tabasco. Pour the filling into the tart shell, and then lay the tomato slices on top of the filling, distributing them evenly.

Bake for 60 to 70 minutes, checking for doneness by sticking a knife into the custard: the knife should come out clean. Serve hot or at room temperature, cut into wedges.

CARAMELIZED
ONION TARTS

MAKES 8 INDIVIDUAL TARTS

These onion tarts are inspired by the classic *pissaladière* from Provence, but with a few twists, including the omission of the traditional anchovies. As you cook the onion, it becomes sweet and delicious. I use store-bought all-butter puff pastry and find it works great and tastes fine. I thaw it in the refrigerator overnight to avoid condensation. These are best the day you make them; keep leftovers wrapped, at room temperature for up to 2 days.

3 tablespoons unsalted butter

2 tablespoons olive oil

1 large onion, thinly sliced

Salt and freshly ground black pepper

All-purpose flour, for rolling

One 16-ounce box frozen all-butter puff pastry, thawed overnight in the refrigerator

4 teaspoons whole-grain mustard

1 medium zucchini

½ teaspoon fresh thyme leaves

24 pitted olives (such as kalamata or Niçoise)

½ cup crumbled feta cheese

Heat the oven to 425 degrees.

Melt the butter with the olive oil in a sauté pan over medium heat. Add the onion, turn the heat down to medium-low, and sauté slowly for about 20 minutes, until the onion is caramelized a bit. Season with just a bit of salt (there's a lot more salt later in the recipe, from the olives and feta) and pepper. Let cool.

Lightly flour a work surface and lay out the 2 pastry sheets. Pass a rolling pin over the pastry sheets just to remove the creases and flatten them. Cut 4 rounds, as large as possible, out of each sheet, and arrange them on two baking sheets. Roll the edges of the rounds in to create a rim. Spread ½ teaspoon of the mustard over the surface of each tart. Divide the onion evenly among the tarts. Cut the zucchini into ¼-inch-thick slices and then cut the slices in half to make half-moons. Tuck the half-moons into the onions, and sprinkle lightly with thyme. Distribute the olives, then the feta, over the tarts.

Bake for 25 to 30 minutes, until the pastry is golden brown on the top and bottom. (Lift it with a spatula to check for doneness.) Serve hot or at room temperature.

POACHED SALMON
WITH CUCUMBER YOGURT

SERVES 4

I blame my stylish aunt Greta from New York. She introduced me to Greek yogurt and now I can't get the stuff out of my mind. I know I sound like a commercial, but you can combine it with almost anything and it's heavenly and thick and creamy and luxurious; and now you can find it in well-stocked supermarkets! Here I use it to bind shredded cucumber to make a refreshing accompaniment to poached salmon fillets. As for that salmon, don't be tempted to cook it longer than I suggest here. It will finish cooking itself as it cools. Believe me, I've cooked it until it looks done only to discover a tight, dry, embarrassing piece of fish later. I'm still making excuses for that incident.

A whole poached side of salmon makes an elegant display on a brunch buffet. If you want to prepare a full side of salmon, double the recipe for the poaching liquid. Double the recipe for the yogurt topping too. Use a fish poacher or a roasting pan to cook the fish. You'll need two spatulas to lift the salmon out of the liquid. It will serve 8 to 10.

FOR THE SALMON

1½ cups dry white wine

1 medium carrot, peeled and thinly sliced

1 small onion, sliced

1 stalk celery, thinly sliced

3 strips lemon zest, removed with a vegetable peeler

10 black peppercorns

1 bay leaf

¼ teaspoon salt

Four 6-ounce, 1-inch-thick salmon fillets, skin off

FOR THE YOGURT TOPPING

1 seedless (English) cucumber, peeled and halved lengthwise

1 cup plain yogurt, preferably Greek yogurt

1 tablespoon snipped fresh dill

Salt and freshly ground black pepper

To make the salmon, in a large saucepan, combine 3 cups water with the wine, carrot, onion, celery, lemon zest, peppercorns, bay leaf, and salt, and bring to a

{CONTINUED ON PAGE 152}

boil over high heat. Then turn the heat down and simmer for 6 minutes, until the carrot is tender. Remove from the heat and cover to keep warm.

Arrange the salmon fillets in a 10-inch sauté pan so they are not touching one another. Pour the hot poaching liquid over the salmon and bring to a simmer over medium heat. Add more water if needed to cover. Cook for just 3 to 4 minutes. The salmon will still be pink and rare in the center. Turn off the heat and let the salmon sit in the liquid for about 10 minutes to finish cooking gently. Then move the pan to the refrigerator and chill the salmon in the poaching liquid for at least 1 hour or up to overnight.

Carefully transfer the salmon (I use a fish spatula, which is slotted and thin) to a serving platter, cover it, and keep it chilled until ready to serve. (Save the poaching liquid for another use; discard the solids.)

To make the yogurt topping, julienne the cucumber, using a Japanese mandoline if you have one; otherwise julienne it in a food processor fitted with the julienne disk. Combine the cucumber, yogurt, and dill in a bowl, and season to taste with salt and pepper. Spoon the yogurt on top of the salmon, and serve.

CORN AND PARMESAN
FRITTERS

MAKES 14 FRITTERS

Being from the Midwest, and specifically from the state that claims the sweet corn capital of the country (it's Hoopeston, Illinois, in case you didn't know), I could eat corn every day—especially during the summer, when it's plentiful and stellar. These fritters do our sweet corn proud and are great paired with fried eggs. Omit the bacon if you want a vegetarian version.

2 tablespoons olive oil

¼ medium onion, diced

1 clove garlic, minced

1 large egg

½ cup whole milk

¼ cup yellow cornmeal

¼ cup all-purpose flour

¼ cup grated Parmesan cheese

⅛ teaspoon baking powder

¼ teaspoon salt

⅛ teaspoon freshly ground black pepper

2 cups corn, frozen or canned (drained)

Canola oil, for frying

Salsa, sour cream, and chopped cooked bacon, for serving

In a nonstick sauté pan, heat the olive oil over medium heat. Add the onion and cook until it is almost translucent, about 3 minutes. Add the garlic and cook for 1 more minute. Using a slotted spoon, remove the onion and garlic from the pan and set aside to cool. Do not clean the pan.

In a mixing bowl, beat the egg and milk together with a fork. Add the cornmeal, flour, Parmesan, baking powder, salt, and pepper, and stir to blend. Stir in the corn.

Add 1 tablespoon canola oil to the oil remaining in the sauté pan, and heat it over medium heat. Spoon fritter batter into the pan to make as many 2½-inch pancakes as will fit comfortably. Let cook until well done on one side, 3 to 4 minutes. Then flip them and cook on the other side for 2 to 3 minutes, until golden brown. Repeat until all the batter is gone, adding more oil to the pan if needed. Arrange the fritters on a serving plate.

Serve warm, topped with salsa, a small dollop of sour cream, and chopped bacon.

GOOEY CAMEMBERT
IN A BOX
WITH CRANBERRY–BLACK PEPPER COMPOTE

SERVES 2 TO 4

This is a great dish if you like contrasting flavors and textures. The tart cranberries and creamy Camembert make an unforgettable pairing. It's also pretty on a buffet, and incredibly easy (really!). Serve it with cornichons, pickled onions, pear slices, dried fruits, and nuts—or any combination thereof.

1½ cups fresh cranberries

⅓ cup sugar

¼ cup port

⅛ teaspoon salt

⅛ teaspoon freshly ground black pepper

One 8-ounce round Camembert cheese, still in the box (about 4½ inches in diameter; domestic is fine)

Sliced baguette or wheat crackers, for serving

For the compote, combine the cranberries, ¼ cup water, and the sugar, port, salt, and pepper in a medium saucepan and bring to a boil over medium heat. Turn the heat down and simmer until the skins of the cranberries pop, 6 to 8 minutes. Let cool, and then transfer the compote to a serving bowl. (You can make this up to 1 week in advance and keep it, covered, in the refrigerator. Serve it chilled or at room temperature.)

For the cheese, remove the lid of the Camembert box and discard any paper wrapping around the cheese. Tie a ribbon or kitchen twine around the circumfer-ence of the box to keep it intact while cooking. Place the box on a plate and micro-wave the cheese for 60 seconds. It may puff up. If it doesn't seem soft and melty, microwave it for 30 more seconds.

Remove the box from the microwave and use a sharp knife to cut three slits through the top rind of the cheese, intersecting at the center, like an asterisk. Peel back the petals of rind to expose the cheese underneath. Serve with the sliced baguette, the compote, and any other accompaniments you like.

GOAT CHEESE AND CHIVE
HASH BROWNS

MAKES ABOUT TEN 2½-INCH CAKES; SERVES 4

These crisp shredded-potato cakes are delicious as an accompaniment to egg dishes. They're not as meaty and cakey as traditional potato pancakes–they're more delicate and sophisticated. Unless, of course, you eat them the way my husband does: with ketchup. I've never tried them that way, but he says the combination is terrific.

3 large potatoes, preferably Yukon Gold

2 large egg whites

½ cup rice flour

½ cup crumbled fresh goat cheese

2 tablespoons chopped fresh chives

1 teaspoon salt

¼ teaspoon freshly ground black pepper

Canola oil, for frying

Grate the potatoes in a food processor, and then rinse them in a colander until the water runs clear. Squeeze them dry, first with your hands and then in a kitchen towel. Put them in a large bowl and stir in the egg whites, rice flour, goat cheese, chives, salt, and pepper.

Heat 3 tablespoons canola oil in a large nonstick sauté pan on medium-high heat. Scoop ½ cup of the potato mixture into the pan and flatten it with the bottom of the measuring cup (or whatever you used to scoop). Repeat, spacing out the cakes but filling the pan as much as possible. Fry the cakes on one side until golden brown, 3 to 4 minutes. Then flip them and fry on the other side until golden brown, 2 to 3 minutes. Remove them from the pan and drain on paper towels. Keep the cakes warm in a 200-degree oven while you fry with the remaining potato mixture. Serve hot.

HOMEMADE PORK AND MAPLE
SAUSAGE PATTIES

SERVES 8

I usually pour maple syrup on my sausage, or dip my sausage in syrup. This recipe takes care of that for me, using the syrup to flavor the homemade breakfast sausage patties. If you have time, mix the ingredients together and let them sit for a day in the refrigerator before cooking them, to bring out the flavors of the spices.

1½ pounds pork shoulder, both lean and fat, cut into ½-inch cubes

¼ cup cold water

2 tablespoons pure maple syrup

1½ teaspoons dried crumbled sage leaves

1½ teaspoons salt

1 teaspoon freshly ground black pepper

½ teaspoon ground nutmeg

Olive oil, for cooking

Place the cubed pork on a plate and freeze it for 10 minutes to firm it up a bit. Then transfer the meat to a food processor and, in batches if necessary (some processor bowls aren't big enough to do it all at once), pulse until the pork pieces are pea-sized. Transfer the meat to a large mixing bowl. Add the cold water, maple syrup, sage, salt, pepper, and nutmeg, and use your hands to mix until well blended. Chill, covered, until you're ready to cook the sausage, preferably overnight and up to 3 days.

Divide the pork mixture into 12 to 16 meatballs, and then flatten them into patties about ½ inch thick. Heat a large skillet or sauté pan over medium heat, and add a touch of olive oil to the pan. Place the patties in the pan and brown them on both sides for about 5 minutes, until cooked through. Drain the patties on a paper towel, if desired, to absorb some of the fat. Serve hot.

CHEESY
CHEDDAR GRITS

SERVES 4

I fell in love with white hominy, a chewy, large-kernel white corn often served in the South, when I used to go down to the Arkansas Folk Festival as a child to perform with my folk-singing dad and brother. (What a funny life I've had!) Hominy can be tossed with bacon for a side dish, or ground into a fine grain for morning grits. This recipe features the grits version, and is great as a hearty breakfast or part of a comforting brunch.

3 cups chicken broth or water

¾ cup instant grits

¼ teaspoon freshly ground black pepper

1 cup grated sharp cheddar cheese

¼ cup grated Parmesan cheese, plus more for serving if desired

1 teaspoon unsalted butter

Salt

Heat the oven to 425 degrees if you'll be serving the grits for a buffet.

Bring the broth to a boil in a medium saucepan. Slowly stir in the grits and pepper, and then reduce the heat to medium-low. Cook, stirring occasionally, until the mixture is thickened and the grits are tender, 5 to 7 minutes. Turn off the heat, add the cheeses and butter, and stir to melt the cheese. Taste for seasoning, and add salt if needed. Serve hot in bowls.

Alternatively, if you're serving this as part of a buffet, pour all the cooked grits into a shallow casserole or gratin dish, sprinkle with a little more Parmesan, and bake for 20 minutes, until slightly browned on top.

GRILLED
PARMESAN AND
BLACK PEPPER POLENTA

SERVES 4 TO 6

I make this polenta often for my kids and serve it right off the stove, while it is still soft. Traditionally, though, polenta (a fine yellow Italian cornmeal) is cooked with chicken stock and herbs and spices, allowed to set, and then cooked again on the grill or pan-fried. For a brunch gathering, I like to make it a day ahead, chill it in sheets, and then cut it up and grill it. The polenta triangles are also great browned in a little butter and olive oil in a skillet. Polenta is simply delicious with cheddar and Parmesan, but you can throw in whatever cheese you like. If you have leftover cheeses that you need to use up, this is the perfect dish to make. It's a nice side dish for a breakfast or brunch of poached eggs and bacon.

3 cups chicken broth or water

¾ cup instant polenta

½ teaspoon freshly ground black pepper

½ cup grated sharp cheddar cheese

½ cup grated Parmesan cheese, plus more for garnish

Salt

1 tablespoon chopped fresh parsley, plus more for garnish

Line a rimmed baking sheet with plastic wrap.

Combine the broth, polenta, and pepper in a medium saucepan and bring to a boil, whisking continually. It will start to thicken and bubble in about 2 minutes. Keep cooking it for another 1 to 2 minutes. Turn off the heat and stir in the cheeses, whisking until they melt. Taste, and add salt if needed. Stir in the parsley.

Pour the polenta into the prepared baking sheet, smooth out the top, lay a piece of plastic wrap on the surface, and chill overnight.

Heat a grill to medium. Turn the chilled polenta out of the baking sheet and cut it into 2- to 3-inch triangles. Grill the polenta triangles on both sides for 2 to 3 minutes, until brown grill marks are visible. Arrange the cooked triangles on a warm serving platter, and sprinkle them with Parmesan and parsley. Serve immediately.

HAM AND VEGETABLE
SCRAPPLE

SERVES 4 TO 6

This old-fashioned dish comes from German settlers in Pennsylvania, New Jersey, Delaware, and Maryland. It's a loaf of cornmeal mush with scraps of pork in it—hence the name—which may not sound especially elegant but belies how good this tastes. The scrapple is generally sliced and then fried, which makes it even better.

1 quart chicken broth or water

1 cup yellow cornmeal

Salt and freshly ground black pepper

2 to 3 tablespoons olive oil

1 small onion, chopped

1 green bell pepper, cored and chopped

1 orange bell pepper, cored and chopped

1 cup cubed ham

Maple syrup, for serving (optional)

Line a loaf pan with plastic wrap, and set it aside.

Combine the broth and the cornmeal in a medium pot and stir to combine. Cook over medium heat, stirring occasionally to keep lumps from forming, until the cornmeal is tender, 30 to 40 minutes. Season with salt and pepper.

Meanwhile, heat 1 tablespoon of the olive oil in a sauté pan and cook the onion for 2 minutes. Add the green and orange bell peppers and contine cooking, adding more olive oil if needed, until the peppers are tender and the onion is translucent, 4 to 5 minutes. Drain off the oil, and stir the sautéed vegetables and the cubed ham into the cooked cornmeal. Pour the cornmeal mixture into the prepared loaf pan. Cover it with plastic wrap and chill it in the refrigerator until set, at least 4 hours and preferably overnight.

Turn the chilled loaf out of the pan and peel off the plastic wrap. Cut it into ½-inch-thick slices. Heat 1 tablespoon olive oil in a skillet over medium heat, and sauté the scrapple slices on both sides until they're a little crusty, 4 to 5 minutes per side. Serve hot, with syrup, if desired.

BEET AND ARTICHOKE SALAD

SALADS & SOUPS

WHEAT BERRY SALAD

FARRO WITH TOMATOES AND PARSLEY

APRICOT CHICKEN SALAD

PEAR WALDORF SALAD

BEET AND ARTICHOKE SALAD

VINAIGRETTE POTATO SALAD

CHICKPEA, CELERY, AND TUNA SALAD

HEIRLOOM TOMATO BISQUE

WATERMELON GAZPACHO

WHEAT BERRY
SALAD

SERVES 4 TO 6

I love the tender crunch of wheat berries—they practically burst in your mouth when you bite into them. They add great texture to so many things, and they stand up well to strong flavors, which is why they work so well with the tuna, cranberries, and feta in this salad. This is delicious as part of a brunch that features both breakfast and lunch dishes.

1 cup wheat berries

½ teaspoon salt, plus more to taste

½ cup diced yellow bell pepper

½ cup diced celery

¼ cup dried cranberries

Two 6-ounce cans water-packed tuna, drained

½ cup crumbled feta cheese

2 hard-boiled eggs, chopped (optional)

2 tablespoons coarsely chopped fresh parsley

½ cup Lemon-Herb Vinaigrette (opposite) or Italian dressing

Freshly ground black pepper

Combine the wheat berries, 1 quart water, and the ½ teaspoon salt in a medium saucepan and bring to a boil. Turn the heat down and simmer for 1 to 1½ hours, until the wheat berries are tender when you bite down on them. Drain well, and let cool.

In a large bowl, toss the cooked wheat berries with the bell pepper, celery, cranberries, tuna, feta, eggs (if using), parsley, dressing, and salt and pepper to taste. Cover, and chill for at least 1 hour and up to 2 days before serving.

LEMON-HERB VINAIGRETTE

MAKES ABOUT 1½ CUPS

This is a great all-purpose dressing to toss with a salad when I'm throwing together whatever is in my vegetable drawer—this brings it all together. The citrus in this vinaigrette cuts the richness from any other dishes you might be serving. I love tossing it with simple greens to serve as a side dish with eggs.

¼ cup fresh lemon juice

¼ cup red wine vinegar

½ teaspoon sugar

2 medium cloves garlic, finely chopped

¼ teaspoon dried oregano

¼ teaspoon chopped fresh parsley

1 cup extra-virgin olive oil

Kosher salt and freshly ground black pepper to taste

In a mixing bowl, whisk together the lemon juice, vinegar, sugar, garlic, oregano, and parsley. Add the oil in a thin stream, whisking constantly until well blended. Add salt and pepper to taste. Use immediately, or refrigerate in a tightly closed jar for up to 3 days. Shake well before using.

FARRO
WITH TOMATOES AND PARSLEY

SERVES 4 TO 6

Farro is a chewy, long-grained, ancient wheat that's high in protein, low in gluten, and delicious. Dress this salad with your favorite Italian dressing, or use the Lemon-Herb Vinaigrette on page 165. Serve it next to an egg dish. I especially like it with Asparagus with Poached Eggs and Parmesan (page 75).

1 cup farro

1 cup chicken broth

1 cup quartered cherry tomatoes or halved grape tomatoes

½ cup diced fennel

½ cup diced seeded cucumber

2 tablespoons coarsely chopped fresh parsley

½ cup Italian dressing or Lemon-Herb Vinaigrette (page 165)

Salt and freshly ground black pepper

Put the farro in a bowl, add 3 cups water, and let soak for 30 minutes.

Drain the farro and place it in a medium saucepan. Add 1½ cups water and the broth, and simmer over medium-low heat for 15 minutes, until the farro is tender when you bite down on it. Drain well, and let cool.

In a large bowl, toss the cooked farro with the tomatoes, fennel, cucumber, parsley, dressing, and salt and pepper to taste. Cover, and chill for at least 1 hour and up to 2 days before serving.

APRICOT
CHICKEN SALAD

SERVES 4 TO 6

Sometimes I buy a roasted chicken and by the time I get halfway through it, I'm ready for something different than just roasted chicken. So I make the rest into chicken salad and it always disappears quickly. Dark meat has more flavor than light, so I recommend using a mixture of the two. I like to use sliced almonds with the skin on, which add even more color to this orange-, red-, and green-speckled salad. You can serve this brunch-time chicken salad with greens or on a slice of bread as an open-face sandwich.

3 cups cubed cooked chicken

½ cup dried apricots, cut into thin strips

½ cup chopped celery

½ cup sliced snow peas or sugar snap peas

¼ cup sliced almonds, toasted (see Note)

¼ to ½ cup mayonnaise, to taste

2 tablespoons fresh lemon juice

1 tablespoon chopped fresh parsley

¼ teaspoon grated orange zest

Salt and freshly ground black pepper

Combine the chicken, apricots, celery, snow peas, almonds, ¼ cup mayonnaise, lemon juice, parsley, and orange zest in a medium bowl, and fold together to combine. Moisten the salad with more mayonnaise if you like a creamier chicken salad, and season it with salt and pepper to taste. Cover, and chill for at least 30 minutes before serving. (The salad keeps for 3 days, covered, in the refrigerator.)

NOTE: *To toast the almonds, spread them in a single layer on a baking sheet and toast in a 375-degree oven for 7 to 10 minutes, stirring after 3 minutes, until golden.*

PEAR WALDORF
SALAD

SERVES 4 TO 6

Waldorf salad, traditionally made with cubed apples, walnuts, and raisins, was a staple in my household when I was growing up. It came from a fancy New York City hotel, the Waldorf-Astoria, so I held it in very high esteem, especially after my family made our first trek to that lively city when I was six, to visit my Aunt Greta. I now think this salad tastes best with in-season fruit—pears, in particular, which are nice paired with fennel and fresh mint.

¼ cup thawed frozen apple juice concentrate

1 tablespoon fresh lemon juice

¼ cup sour cream

¼ cup mayonnaise

1 pinch salt

4 grinds freshly ground black pepper

3 ripe pears, unpeeled, cored and diced

¼ cup diced fennel

¼ cup chopped celery

½ cup raisins

½ cup walnut pieces

2 fresh mint leaves, shredded

In a large bowl, whisk together the apple juice concentrate, lemon juice, sour cream, mayonnaise, salt, and pepper. Add the pears, fennel, celery, raisins, walnuts, and mint. Toss gently, just until combined, and serve immediately.

BEET AND ARTICHOKE
SALAD

SERVES 4 TO 6

I love Green City Market, Chicago's organic and sustainable farmer's market. When I'm there in late summer and fall, I usually buy every different kind of beet I can find. My favorite varieties of late are Golden Globe, Bull's Blood, and Candy Striped. I love to roast or boil them, cut them up, and keep them in the refrigerator to add to salads or just to snack on. This looks beautiful and colorful as part of a brunch buffet.

FOR THE SALAD

- 3 large beets
- 1 tablespoon olive oil
- Salt and freshly ground black pepper
- One 14-ounce can or jar artichoke hearts
- 1 cup frozen peas, thawed
- 1 cup cubed peeled jicama
- ½ cup crumbled fresh goat cheese

FOR THE VINAIGRETTE

- ¼ cup fresh orange juice
- ¼ cup red wine vinegar
- 2 tablespoons fresh lemon juice
- ½ teaspoon sugar
- 2 medium cloves garlic, finely chopped
- 1 teaspoon Dijon mustard
- 1 cup extra-virgin olive oil
- Salt and freshly ground black pepper
- 2 tablespoons fresh parsley leaves

Heat the oven to 450 degrees.

To make the salad, trim the tops and roots off the beets and wash the beets. Place them on a piece of foil, sprinkle them with the olive oil and salt and pepper to taste, and gather the foil to make a bundle. Roast until tender, 1¼ to 1½ hours (or longer, if the beets are very large). Let the beets cool in the foil.

Meanwhile, drain the artichoke hearts and quarter them. Combine them with the peas and jicama in a medium bowl.

{*CONTINUED ON PAGE 172*}

When the beets are cool, peel them and cut them into chunks about the same size as the artichoke pieces. Place the cut-up beets in a separate medium bowl.

To make the vinaigrette, whisk together the orange juice, vinegar, lemon juice, sugar, garlic, and mustard in a bowl. Add the oil in a thin stream, whisking constantly until well blended. Add salt and pepper to taste, and whisk in the parsley leaves.

Pour half of the vinaigrette over the beets and the other half over the artichoke mixture. Cover both bowls and let marinate in the refrigerator for at least 1 hour or overnight.

Just before serving, combine the beets (they may give off some color) and the artichoke mixture in a serving bowl and sprinkle the goat cheese over the top.

VINAIGRETTE
POTATO SALAD

SERVES 6 TO 8

I usually find potato salads too creamy and too mushy for my taste. That's where this recipe comes in: I pair the potatoes with crunchy fennel, corn, and bacon and dress everything in nothing but a lightly flavored fresh dill vinaigrette.

6 medium Yukon Gold potatoes, peeled and cut in half crosswise

1 tablespoon olive oil

Kernels from 3 ears corn

Salt and freshly ground black pepper

1 cup diced fennel

½ cup chopped cooked bacon

About ¾ cup Dill Vinaigrette (opposite)

Put the potatoes in a large saucepan and cover with salted water. Bring the water to a boil and cook the potatoes until they are fork-tender, about 20 minutes. Drain in a colander and let cool. Cut into 1-inch pieces.

Heat the olive oil in a nonstick sauté pan, and sauté the corn kernels until they are just starting to brown, 3 to 4 minutes. Season with salt and pepper. Set aside to cool.

In a large bowl, combine the potatoes, corn, fennel, and bacon. Pour the dressing over the vegetables and fold them together carefully. Cover, and chill for at least 1 hour and up to 2 days before serving.

DILL VINAIGRETTE

MAKES ABOUT 1¼ CUPS

- 3 tablespoons fresh lemon juice
- 3 tablespoons red wine vinegar
- ½ teaspoon sugar
- 1 tablespoon Dijon mustard
- 2 medium cloves garlic, finely chopped
- 2 teaspoons snipped fresh dill
- ¼ teaspoon chopped fresh parsley
- ¾ cup extra-virgin olive oil

  Salt and freshly ground black pepper

In a mixing bowl, whisk together the lemon juice, vinegar, sugar, mustard, garlic, dill, and parsley. Add the oil in a thin stream, whisking constantly until well blended. Add salt and pepper to taste. Use immediately, or refrigerate in a tightly closed jar for up to 3 days. Shake well before using.

CHICKPEA, CELERY, AND TUNA
SALAD

SERVES 4 TO 6

My husband, Jimmy, loves chickpeas. He's always picking up a can or two at the store, whether we already have them in the pantry or not . . . just in case. His favorite tossed salads start with chickpeas (who needs greens?) and end with whatever leftovers in the fridge need finishing. He makes a game out of using up as many remnants in cans and jars, and as many errant vegetables as possible. We actually call him "the finisher." This is a very colorful and tasty salad, Jimmy style, that is perfect for an informal family brunch with a mix of sweet and savory treats.

One 15-ounce can chickpeas, rinsed and drained

2 medium yellow tomatoes, quartered

½ cup diced celery

½ cup diced seeded cucumber

2 hard-boiled eggs, chopped

One 6-ounce can light tuna packed in water, drained

2 tablespoons coarsely chopped fresh parsley

2 tablespoons capers (optional)

½ teaspoon grated lemon zest

½ cup Italian dressing or Lemon-Herb Vinaigrette (page 165)

Salt and freshly ground black pepper

Put the chickpeas in a large bowl and toss with the tomatoes, celery, cucumber, eggs, tuna, parsley, capers (if using), lemon zest, and dressing. Season with salt and pepper, and toss again. Cover, and chill for at least 30 minutes or overnight before serving.

HEIRLOOM
TOMATO BISQUE

SERVES 4 TO 6

At the end of the Midwest summer, all the tomatoes get picked (and put to work) before the first frost. In my house, this recipe is where many of them end up. I've made this soup with all kinds of heirloom varieties, including Pink Ping Pongs, Black Zebras, Boxcar Willies, and a newly named variety: the Julia Child. (Didn't you always want to have a tomato named after you? She has a rose too. It's yellow.) You could serve this hot or chilled in demitasse cups, accompanied by a Panini Finger Sandwich (page 132) or topped with a little spoonful of Pesto (page 139).

1 tablespoon olive oil

1 medium onion, chopped

3 cloves garlic, sliced

2 pounds ripe heirloom tomatoes, halved, seeded, and chopped

8 fresh basil leaves

1 sprig fresh thyme

2 cups canned or bottled tomato juice

1 cup chicken broth

Salt and freshly ground black pepper

2 cups heavy cream

In a large pot, heat the oil over medium heat. Add the onion and cook, stirring occasionally, until translucent, about 5 minutes. Add the garlic and sauté for 1 minute. Add the tomatoes, basil, and thyme and cook for about 10 minutes to soften the tomatoes and release some of their juices. Add the tomato juice and chicken broth, and simmer for 30 to 40 minutes to thicken. Remove the thyme sprig and season to taste with salt and pepper.

Let the mixture cool slightly, and then puree it, in batches, in a blender or food processor. If you want the soup even smoother, strain it through a strainer, pushing on it with the back of a spoon to get all the liquid. Taste again for seasoning, and then stir in the cream. Reheat if serving hot, but do not boil. (This soup can be made a day ahead and chilled, covered. It can also be frozen, in an airtight container, for up to 2 months.)

WATERMELON
GAZPACHO

SERVES 4 TO 6

The first time I hosted a dinner party was when my parents came to visit me halfway through my first semester of art school in Cleveland. I served tomato gazpacho, an easy soup made in the blender, and offered ingredients at the table to stir into the soup. I got creative and had things like cottage cheese, croutons, and popcorn, as well as the traditional vegetables like cucumbers and peppers. And I've been playing with different versions of gazpacho ever since. Here's the latest, thirtysomething years later. This watermelon version is somewhere between sweet and savory—perfect for brunch—and looks gorgeous in glass bowls or cups.

4 cups watermelon cubes, seeds removed as much as possible

Sugar, to taste

½ cup diced seedless (English) cucumber

½ orange or red bell pepper, diced

1 green apple, cored and diced

¼ cup pomegranate seeds

½ cup cubed fresh mozzarella

Put the watermelon cubes in a blender and pulse briefly to puree, leaving some texture to them. Transfer the watermelon to a container with a pour spout. Taste, and sweeten with a little sugar if it's too tart.

To serve, pour the watermelon soup into clear bowls, glasses, or mugs. Garnish each serving with a bit of cucumber, bell pepper, apple, pomegranate seeds, and mozzarella. Alternatively, set the bowls of soup on a buffet, next to small serving bowls containing the vegetables, fruit, and cheese, and let people garnish their own soup.

ROASTED PEARS AND RHUBARB WITH ORANGE

FRUITS
&
CONDIMENTS

LEMON CREAM

BANANAS FOSTER

STRAWBERRIES IN SYRUP

ROASTED PEARS AND RHUBARB WITH ORANGE

FRESH FRUIT SALAD

THREE-BERRY COMPOTE

CHOCOLATE-HAZELNUT SPREAD

NANA'S STRAWBERRY PRESERVES

APRICOT GINGER JAM

HOT OR COLD HONEY BUTTER

FRUIT BUTTERS

FLAVORED CREAM CHEESES

SPICY HORSERADISH MUSTARD

LEMON
CREAM

MAKES ABOUT 2 CUPS

This mouthwatering cream is great for dolloping on French toast, pancakes, fruit salad, or oatmeal, or for schmearing on scones or muffins.

2 large eggs

½ cup sugar

Grated zest of ½ lemon

⅓ cup fresh lemon juice

Ice cubes

2 tablespoons unsalted butter

½ cup heavy cream, chilled

Bring about 2 inches of water to a simmer in a large saucepan.

In a mixer fitted with the whisk attachment (or using a hand mixer), whip the eggs and sugar together until light yellow and fluffy. Mix in the lemon zest and lemon juice. Rest the mixing bowl on the saucepan, with the bowl's base resting above, not in, the simmering water (pour out some water if necessary). Cook, whisking often, until the mixture is warm, thickened, and pudding-like, about 10 minutes.

Meanwhile, fill a large bowl with ice and cover it with cold water.

Remove the mixing bowl from the hot water and whisk in the butter until melted. Rest the bottom of the bowl in the ice bath and let cool, stirring the mixture occasionally, until it is cool and thick.

In a mixer fitted with the whisk attachment (or using a hand mixer), whip the cream until stiff. Fold it into the cooled lemon custard. Cover, and refrigerate for at least 1 hour or for up to 3 days.

BANANAS FOSTER

SERVES 4

This is a classic New Orleans topping for ice cream, but these bananas are also great for dressing up pancakes, waffles, or even a humble bowl of oatmeal. When I was a waitress (there was a time when I couldn't get a job as a cook for lack of experience!) at a little French place in Cleveland Heights, Ohio, called Au Provence, we did a lot of tableside service, and Bananas Foster was one of the items in my repertoire. We flambéed it with banana liqueur, but I don't even know if they make that stuff anymore, and I hate to make you buy a whole bottle just for this one recipe. (I wouldn't; I'm way too much of a cheapskate!) Brandy or another dark spirit works just fine and there's no need to flambé it.

4 tablespoons unsalted butter

½ cup sugar

½ vanilla bean, split, or ½ teaspoon pure vanilla extract

1 cinnamon stick

1 tablespoon brandy or other brown spirit (cognac, whiskey, rum, etc.)

1 tablespoon fresh lemon juice

2 bananas, sliced

Melt the butter in a small saucepan over medium heat until slightly bubbly. Add the sugar and stir it in with a wooden spoon. Add the vanilla bean (but not the extract, if that's what you're using) and the cinnamon stick and stir to combine and release the vanilla seeds. Continue cooking until the sugar starts to caramelize, or turn a light amber color, 2 to 3 minutes.

Carefully stir in the brandy and lemon juice, and continue cooking until the syrup becomes caramel-smooth, 2 to 3 minutes. Add the banana slices (and vanilla extract, if using) and swirl to coat them in the hot syrup and warm them, about 1 minute. Serve immediately.

STRAWBERRIES
IN SYRUP

SERVES 4 TO 6

I love tossing cut strawberries in sugar to encourage them to release their tasty natural juices and make their own ruby-colored syrup. If you want to add other berries for color and textural contrast, go ahead. Just make sure they are ripe and flavorful. Try adding the pepper—it gives a great kick.

1 pint strawberries, hulled and roll cut (see note)

2 tablespoons sugar

⅛ teaspoon freshly ground black pepper (optional)

Combine the strawberries, sugar, and pepper (if using) in a bowl, and toss. The fruit will start to release its juices, which will combine with the sugar and dissolve it. Cover, and chill until ready to serve, at least 30 minutes and up to 8 hours.

THE ROLL CUT

A roll cut, sometimes called a Japanese roll cut, is a technique often used to cut cucumbers or carrots. It's also great for cutting strawberries into bite-sized pieces that won't stick together in a bowl the way slices do. Cut the first slice with your knife at a slight angle (tip at 11 o'clock and handle at 5 o'clock). Keeping the knife at that same angle, roll the strawberry (or whatever you're cutting) a quarter-turn and slice down again. Continue until the fruit or vegetable is entirely sliced into angular-looking chunks.

ROASTED PEARS
AND RHUBARB WITH ORANGE

SERVES 4 TO 6

A few years ago there was an explosion in the availability of heirloom varieties of apples in our grocery stores, and now the same thing is happening with pears. Whatever kind you buy, stick your nose right up to them and sniff to find the fragrant ones—they'll have the best flavor. If the old standbys are your only options, Bartlett would be my choice. I've included a recipe here for my favorite crunchy topping to serve on anything plump and juicy. You can make the topping up to a week in advance, but if it's too much trouble, you can just leave it off. Try serving this next to Almond Ciabatta French Toast (page 90).

4 medium pears, ripe but firm

4 stalks rhubarb, trimmed and washed

½ cup orange juice

2 tablespoons honey

2 tablespoons light-bodied red wine (such as Beaujolais or whatever you have open)

½ cup packed light brown sugar

1 vanilla bean, split (optional)

2 teaspoons cornstarch

½ teaspoon ground cinnamon

Crunchy Almond Topping (optional; opposite)

Heat the oven to 400 degrees.

Quarter and core the pears (do not peel them). Cut the rhubarb into 1-inch sections.

In a large bowl, combine the orange juice, honey, wine, brown sugar, vanilla bean (if using), cornstarch, and cinnamon. Add the pears and rhubarb, and toss to coat. Pour into a casserole or gratin dish and bake until tender, 35 to 40 minutes, basting occasionally with a turkey baster to moisten the fruit.

When the fruit is done, remove it from the oven, and if you're making the crunchy almond topping, reduce the oven temperature to 350 degrees. Serve the fruit warm or at room temperature, with the almonds sprinkled on top, if desired.

CRUNCHY ALMOND TOPPING

MAKES ¾ CUP

- ¾ cup sliced almonds
- ¼ cup sugar
- 1 large egg white, lightly beaten

Heat the oven to 350 degrees.

Toss the almonds and sugar together, then add the egg white, and mix well to coat the almonds. Lightly grease a baking sheet and spread the almond mixture on it. Bake the almonds, turning them with a spatula after 5 minutes, until they are golden brown and caramelized, 10 to 12 minutes. Let cool. Store in an airtight container at room temperature for up to 1 week.

FRESH FRUIT SALAD

SERVE 4 TO 6

Pineapple juice is high in acid, which helps to keep the fruit from oxidizing and turning brown. A hint of mint and lemon adds vibrant flavor to this salad. I like to use a roll cut, usually reserved for carrots, when I cut strawberries and bananas.

1 cup seedless green grapes, halved

½ cantaloupe, seeded, peeled, and cubed

1 pint strawberries, hulled and roll cut (see page 185)

½ pint blueberries

2 bananas, roll cut (see page 185)

2 ripe pears, unpeeled, cored and cut into chunks

1 cup pineapple juice

2 fresh mint leaves, thinly sliced

½ teaspoon grated lemon zest

In a large bowl, toss the grapes, cantaloupe, strawberries, blueberries, bananas, and pears with the pineapple juice. Fold in the mint and lemon zest. Cover, and chill for at least 30 minutes and up to 8 hours.

THREE-BERRY COMPOTE

SERVES 4 TO 6

Cooking berries for just a few minutes brings out the jammy flavors in the fruit and makes a nice, simple summery topping for just about anything. Use it on pancakes, in yogurt, in crêpes, or on oatmeal.

1 pint strawberries, hulled and roll cut (see page 185)

1 pint blueberries

1 pint raspberries

2 tablespoons light brown sugar

½ teaspoon grated orange zest

⅛ teaspoon pure vanilla extract

In a medium saucepan, combine the strawberries, blueberries, raspberries, brown sugar, orange zest, and 2 tablespoons water. Bring to a boil, then immediately turn off the heat. Let cool slightly, and then stir in the vanilla extract. Serve warm or chilled. (The compote will keep for up to 5 days, covered, in the refrigerator.)

CHOCOLATE-HAZELNUT
SPREAD

MAKES ABOUT 1½ CUPS

On a trip to Italy, I became addicted to Nutella, a popular decadent chocolate-hazelnut spread. I can't always find it in stores here, so I created my own version of it. It's perfect for spreading in crêpes or on toasted pound cake, or as a topping for French toast or waffles. My kids like to eat it with a banana—a little bit with each bite!

1 cup hazelnuts, toasted and peeled (see note, page 192)

2 tablespoons canola oil

2 tablespoons confectioners' sugar

1 tablespoon unsweetened cocoa powder

½ teaspoon pure vanilla extract

12 ounces milk chocolate, chopped and melted (see note, page 192)

Grind the hazelnuts well in a food processor to make a paste. Add the oil, confectioners' sugar, cocoa powder, and vanilla and continue processing. Add the melted chocolate and blend well. Strain the mixture through a fine-mesh strainer into a bowl, to remove any large nut pieces. The mixture will be thin and a little warm. Pour it into a jar and let it cool and thicken slightly. This spread keeps for a month in an airtight container at room temperature.

PEELING HAZELNUTS

To remove the skins from hazelnuts, heat the oven to 350 degrees. Toast the hazelnuts in one layer on a baking sheet for 12 to 15 minutes, until the nuts are browned and the skins are slightly blistered. Wrap them in a tea towel and rub (and rub) to remove all the loose skin. Not all of the skin will loosen enough to be removed, and that's fine. Let cool before chopping.

MELTING CHOCOLATE

To melt chocolate, first chop the chocolate into pieces. Place it in the top of a double boiler and melt it over barely simmering water. If you don't have a double boiler, set a metal or heatproof glass bowl over a saucepan with about an inch of water in the bottom, and heat the water to barely simmering. The bottom of the bowl should not touch the water. No matter what equipment you're using, do not let the water bubble or boil, as this could scorch the chocolate. Stir the chocolate frequently as it is melting, and do not cover it at any time—drops of water could accumulate on the lid, and if they touch the chocolate, it could seize up and stiffen.

To melt chocolate in a microwave oven, put the chopped chocolate in a glass bowl and heat it on medium power for 1 minute. Stir the chocolate, then continue heating as necessary in increments of 30 seconds or less. Stop when there are still a few lumps of chocolate remaining, and stir until they are melted.

NANA'S
STRAWBERRY PRESERVES

MAKES ABOUT 1 PINT

My coauthor, Christie, says her late grandmother, Betty Craven (also known as Nana Banana), used to make the best strawberry preserves. Simple and bursting with large pieces of fruit, and brightened with a touch of citrus, they were always better than supermarket jams. Use fresh, local, organic strawberries if possible—with such a simple concoction, the quality of the ingredients really matters.

2 pints strawberries, hulled and halved

1 cup sugar

½ teaspoon grated lemon zest

2 teaspoons fresh lemon juice

Put the strawberries in a medium saucepan and mash them slightly with a fork. Heat them over medium heat for 8 minutes. Turn the heat down to low and stir in the sugar until dissolved. Stir in the lemon zest and juice. Turn the heat back up to medium and cook for 20 to 25 minutes, until thick. Pour into a jar and let cool. The preserves keep in a tightly lidded jar in the refrigerator for up to 2 weeks.

APRICOT GINGER JAM

I love making jam, giving jam, and eating jam. Here's one of my favorites to make in the summer, when apricots are plentiful in the Midwest. I get apricots from my friend Pete Klein, who owns Seedlings Farm in South Haven, Michigan. (We call him Farmer Pete.) Last year a late frost in the spring killed off all the apricot buds, so we went without. I plan to make up for it this coming summer.

2½ pounds ripe fresh apricots, pitted and quartered (about 4 cups)

2 tablespoons grated fresh ginger

⅓ cup fresh lemon juice

5¾ cups sugar

½ teaspoon unsalted butter

3 ounces (6 tablespoons) liquid pectin, such as Certo liquid fruit pectin

In a large pot, combine the apricots, ginger, lemon juice, and sugar and stir to combine. Add the butter. Bring to a full rolling boil over high heat, stirring gently but constantly. Once the mixture boils, quickly stir in the pectin. Return to a boil and boil for 1 minute exactly, stirring the whole time. Then turn off the heat, and use a spoon to skim off any foam on the surface. Ladle the hot jam into jars. Let cool; then cover, and store the jam in the refrigerator for up to 2 weeks.

HOT OR COLD
HONEY BUTTER

MAKES ½ CUP

This is great to have in the fridge to dress up morning pancakes, waffles, or French toast. Or just spread it on toast! Look for local honey, which has wonderful flavor.

¼ cup (1 stick) unsalted butter, at room temperature

1 pinch salt

1 tablespoon honey

In a bowl, beat the butter with a wooden spoon. Then mix in the salt and honey. Pack the honey butter into ramekins, and serve it at room temperature; or warm it in a small saucepan over low heat (or in the microwave for 10 seconds at a time) until melted, and serve it hot.

FRUIT BUTTERS

MAKES ½ CUP

Making flavored butter is *so* easy and a great way to gussy up store-bought baked goods. All you have to do is take a stick of butter out of the refrigerator and let it come almost to room temperature. Then whip it in a food processor, or in a mixer with a whip attachment, to aerate it and make it fluffy and then add the flavoring. After the butter and the flavoring are thoroughly blended together, use a rubber spatula to pack the flavored butter into a ceramic ramekin. Smooth the surface and chill the butter until you're almost ready to serve. Remove it from the refrigerator 15 to 30 minutes before serving time, so it's easy to spread.

ORANGE BUTTER
Whip ½ cup (1 stick) unsalted butter with
½ teaspoon grated orange zest.

LEMON BUTTER
Whip ½ cup (1 stick) unsalted butter with
½ teaspoon grated lemon zest.

STRAWBERRY BUTTER
Puree 2 hulled medium-sized strawberries
with ½ cup (1 stick) unsalted butter.

RASPBERRY BUTTER
Puree 8 to 10 raspberries with ½ cup (1 stick)
unsalted butter.

BLACKBERRY BUTTER
Puree 5 to 6 blackberries, and whip with
½ cup (1 stick) unsalted butter.

FLAVORED
CREAM CHEESES

MAKES 1 CUP

Flavored cream cheese is as easy to make as flavored butter. And even quicker, because though you'll want to let the cream cheese warm up a bit before whipping it, you don't need to let it come to room temperature. Add whatever items you like to flavor it; here are a few of my favorites. Serve flavored cream cheese in demitasse cups or mini glass bowls with bagels, muffins, or soft pretzels.

PESTO CREAM CHEESE

Whip 8 ounces cream cheese with 1 tablespoon pesto.

LEMON-THYME CREAM CHEESE

Whip 8 ounces cream cheese with 1 teaspoon grated lemon zest and $\frac{1}{2}$ teaspoon fresh thyme leaves.

AUTUMN SPICE CREAM CHEESE

Whip 8 ounces cream cheese with $\frac{1}{2}$ teaspoon ground cinnamon, $\frac{1}{4}$ teaspoon ground ginger, $\frac{1}{8}$ teaspoon ground nutmeg, and $\frac{1}{8}$ teaspoon ground cloves.

SPICY HORSERADISH MUSTARD

MAKES 1½ CUPS

There are so many kinds of mustard you can make—here's a good one to start with. You can omit the horseradish and garlic for a more mellow experience, or change the vinegar to a red wine vinegar for a sharper flavor. Or try to find whole brown mustard seeds and add those for another variation. Have fun with this one.

¼ cup dry mustard

2 tablespoons whole yellow mustard seeds

¾ cup cider vinegar

1 clove garlic, minced

1 tablespoon prepared horseradish

1 teaspoon salt

½ teaspoon light brown sugar

Combine the dry mustard, mustard seeds, vinegar, and ¼ cup water in a jar. Add the garlic, horseradish, salt, and brown sugar and let sit, covered, for 48 hours in the refrigerator.

Pour the mixture into a food processor and blend until smooth, about 2 minutes. Then pour it into a small glass jar, cover it tightly, and refrigerate for up to 1 month. The flavor improves after aging in the refrigerator for a week or two.

MENUS

NEW YEAR'S DAY BRUNCH

Tangerine–Pink Grapefruit Juice
(page 32)

Poached Salmon with
Cucumber Yogurt (page 150)

Wheat Berry Salad (page 164)

Fresh Fruit Salad (page 188)

SUMMER WEEKEND BRUNCH

Flavored Lemonades (pages 29-30)

Ginger Scones with
Peaches and Cream (page 106)

Oven-Roasted Tomato, Niçoise Olive,
Mozzarella, and Goat Cheese Quiche
(page 54)

Three-Berry Compote (page 189)

GOING AWAY PARTY BRUNCH

Gale's 3-Alarm Bloody Mary
(page 37)

Mini Potato Pancakes with Smoked
Salmon (page 131)

Herbed Mini Popovers (page 128)

Cheddar, Pancetta, and Spinach
Frittata (page 50)

Bacon

BRUNCH WITH THE KIDS

Hot Cocoa with Brown Sugar
(page 22)

Peanut Butter and Jelly
Turnovers (page 119)

Buttermilk Pancakes (page 80)

Homemade Pork and Maple Sausage
Patties (page 158)

Fresh Fruit Salad (page 188)

CELEBRATORY CHAMPAGNE BRUNCH

Champagne
(have orange juice on hand to make mimosas)

Champagne and Cranberry
with Mint (page 33)

Heirloom Tomato Bisque
(page 177)

Spinach and Cheddar Soufflé
(page 73)

Roasted Pears and Rhubarb
with Orange (page 186)

BRIDAL SHOWER BRUNCH

Champagne Pimm's Cup (page 34)

Gougères (page 126)

Watermelon Gazpacho (page 179)

Panini Finger Sandwiches (page 132)

Hand-Formed Pear and
Almond Tartlets (page 120)

BABY SHOWER BRUNCH

Banana-Raspberry Smoothie
(page 26)

Granola-Peach Parfait (page 103)

Basic Waffles (page 86)

Lemon Cream (page 182)

MOTHER'S DAY BRUNCH

Pineapple-Blueberry Smoothie
(page 27)

Apricot Chicken Salad (page 169)

Asparagus with Poached Eggs
and Parmesan (page 75)

Quick Pear Streusel
Coffee Cake (page 111)

Strawberries in Syrup
(page 185)

THE IN-LAWS ARE COMING! BRUNCH

Orange-Lime Juice
with Grenadine
(page 31)

Baked Eggs in Ham Cups
(page 68)

Spiced Apple-Raisin Turnovers
(page 117)

HOLIDAY OPEN HOUSE BRUNCH

White Hot Chocolate with Orange
(page 24)

Tangerine–Pink Grapefruit Juice
(page 32)

Fried Quail Eggs on
Eggnog French Toast
(page 140)

Gooey Camembert in a Box with
Cranberry–Black Pepper Compote
(page 154)

Asparagus, Black Truffle,
and Gouda Quiche (page 54)

Cranberry Angel-Food Muffins
(page 116)

EQUIPMENT & INGREDIENTS

Making brunch does not require much in the way of fancy equipment or ingredients. That said, it can be helpful to have some essentials on hand. I refer to the specific things you'll need for each dish in its respective recipe, but here are some general thoughts on the basics of a brunch kitchen.

EQUIPMENT

PIE, QUICHE, TART, AND CAKE PANS: An assortment of round pans comes in handy for making quiches, galettes, and tortas.

MUFFIN TINS AND POPOVER PANS: I have muffin pans in a range of sizes, from mini to extra-large. I love to mix up the size of muffins I make: sometimes giant ones are a decadent morning treat; at other times mini muffins round out a bread basket beautifully. A muffin tin can sub for a popover pan when making popovers, but only the real thing will give you the height popovers are known for.

SOUFFLÉ DISH AND RAMEKINS: A soufflé dish is a round ceramic dish with straight sides that allow a soufflé to puff up perfectly. Ramekins are basically mini soufflé dishes that are great for baking individual bread puddings and other treats and for serving flavored butters and cream cheeses. They also work well for coddling eggs.

OMELET PAN: Generally I'm not a fan of nonstick pans for regular cooking, but I keep two nonstick pans in the house for omelets and crêpes. (I'm careful never to walk away from them when they're on the stove, so I can make sure they don't overheat; as studies have shown that's not so healthy.) Omelets are so much easier to make if you're not worrying about your eggs sticking to the pan! Look for a pan with low, curved sides, a flat bottom that's 8 to 10 inches in diameter, and a long heatproof handle.

SKILLET: For making frittatas, you'll want a bigger pan than you'd use for omelets, also nonstick—a solid, heavyweight, 12-inch ovenproof skillet. You can also make scrambled and fried eggs in a skillet.

GRIDDLE: For making a bunch of pancakes or French toast, this cooking surface is tough to beat. A large skillet works too, but if you have space to store a griddle that fits over two burners (or to install one with your range), I highly recommend it.

WAFFLE IRON: Well, you can't make waffles without one. And who doesn't want to make waffles sometimes? I have an electric waffle iron that you can flip over once you've poured the batter in, and then make a second waffle on the other side.

PANINI GRILL: This is required for only one recipe in this book, the Panini Finger Sandwiches, but I love my panini press so much that I want you to have one too. It makes truly fantastic sandwiches.

JUICER: Freshly squeezed juice is a much less daunting prospect if you don't have to juice the fruit by hand! I have two vintage hand-crank juicers and one electric juicer. If you're buying electric, I recommend not getting one that's too fast or powerful. Juicing fruit is a great job for guests or kids—you can put the cut fruit out for them in a bowl, and have another bowl ready for the juiced "skulls"—so you don't want a juicer that's hard to understand or scary. And make sure the parts are easy to clean.

FOOD PROCESSOR: Shredding potatoes for potato pancakes is a cinch in a food processor. So is grating cheese, grinding nuts for Chocolate-Hazelnut Spread, and making pesto.

BLENDER: When you want a smoothie, all you need to do is toss frozen fruit in a blender with a few other ingredients (a little juice and yogurt, for example), and it's ready in seconds.

PITCHERS: I use pitchers of all sizes for so many things at brunch. I serve freshly squeezed juices in pretty glass pitchers; I make large batches of cocktails, such as my 3-Alarm Bloody Mary, in pitchers; and I use measuring cups with pour spouts for pancake, popover, and waffle batter (these make life easier for me, and for my kids if they're helping).

WHISK: A thin wire whisk is invaluable for lightly beating eggs, preparing batter for popovers, mixing up custard for French toast, and so much more.

WOODEN SPOON: This is the best implement for stirring eggs gently in the pan while they're cooking, especially if you're using a nonstick pan. It's also great for preparing batters that don't require an electric mixer, especially when you want some lumps remaining, as in pancake batter.

SPATULAS: Have a heatproof silicone one for rolling omelets out of the pan and for gently folding ingredients into muffin and quick-bread batters. Use a metal one for flipping pancakes and French toast.

TONGS: I don't think I could cook without tongs. They are like an extension of my body—I keep them in my back pocket and use them all the time. Try them for turning bacon, getting asparagus out of the water after you blanch it, removing potstickers from their pan, or grabbing pretty much anything.

ZESTERS: Lemon and orange zests are essential ingredients in my cooking, both sweet and savory, and zesters are ideal for attaining a perfect zest. You could also use the small holes on a box or hand grater (carefully, because you are cutting a tough peel and don't want to cut yourself) or a vegetable peeler (mince the pieces of peel into small shreds). For very fine grating, use a fine Microplane.

INGREDIENTS

EGGS: I'm a cheapskate, so I don't buy organic all the time. But I do at least try to look for free-range brown eggs, which have the most flavor and a more colorful, intense yolk. Places raising chickens that lay brown eggs are generally doing other good things like making sure their chickens and eggs are hormone-free.

It's easiest to separate eggs when they are cold. After the eggs are separated, for the best results let the whites warm up a bit before whipping them, and be sure to whip them in a spotlessly clean (no fat or oil residue, please), dry bowl.

MILK: In many recipes, you can use anything from skim milk to whole milk and achieve fine results. Where whole milk is necessary, I specify that.

BUTTER: I almost always use unsalted butter so I can control the amount of salt in the recipe. Unsalted butter tends to be fresher too, because salt acts as a preservative and salted butter can sit around in grocery stores longer. For the recipes in this book, I use only unsalted butter.

CHEESE: Find a cheese shop or a grocery store with a good-quality cheese section to help guide you in what to buy. There's a shop near me with an amazing cheese selection, and I'm confident that anything I buy there is going to be right. They've gone to the trouble of figuring out what is really good, so I don't have to. This is helpful for cheese and any other ingredient, really: Patronize stores where the staff is passionate about ingredients. Your support will help enable them to keep doing what they do.

FLOUR: Use unbleached flour, which hasn't gone through the bleaching process and thus been stripped of practically all its nutrients. Unless I specify otherwise, use all-purpose flour.

PUFF PASTRY: Frozen all-butter puff pastry is one convenience product I rely on often at home to make turnovers, tortas, and more. To avoid condensation, thaw it overnight in the refrigerator instead of at room temperature. When you unfold it, roll it slightly with a rolling pin to smooth out creases and cracks. If it gets sticky, return it to the freezer for 15 minutes or so to firm it up.

FRUITS AND VEGETABLES: Whenever possible, buy produce that's in season locally instead of produce that's out of season or needs to be shipped from thousands of miles away. Fruit tastes better when it's super-fresh and in season, and it's more economical that way. It's also better for you—the longer produce travels and sits from the moment it was picked, the more nutrients it loses. And when we're buying fruits and vegetables, we should look at how many "food miles" they have traveled (how far have they come, and how much fossil fuel was used to get them to us). The less fossil fuel we use, the better for the environment.

ACKNOWLEDGMENTS

Thank you to my friends, family, and colleagues, who inspire me—especially Jane Dystel; Christie Matheson; Ben Fink; Rica Allannic; my dad, Bob Gand; my late (in both senses of the word) mother, Myrna Gand; Grandma Elsie Grossman; my mother-in-law, Vita Seidita; Ina Pinkney the Breakfast Queen and her heavenly hots; Lana Rae; Judy Anderson and her family; Kathy Skutecki; Marthe Young; Greta and Robert Pearson; Karen Katz and her family; my assistant, Jeffrey Ward; Rick Tramonto; Rich Melman; Edy our nanny; Karen and Ron Filbert (who bottle my Gale's Root Beer for me); Gio's sixth-grade teacher, Ms. Mary Courtney; and Peter Klein, my favorite local farmer.

And a special thanks to P. I. Tchaikovsky for providing me with an hour every day to work without feeling that I am neglecting my little girls, because they are always so happy watching their DVD of The Nutcracker ballet.

—GALE GAND

Gale Gand, what a pleasure it is to work with you! Thank you for sharing a wonderful book-creating experience with me. Huge thanks to Jane Dystel, Stacey Click, Rica Allannic, and Ben Fink. Thanks to Nana Banana for the preserves recipe and so much more. And thanks to Will, always and for everything.

—CHRISTIE MATHESON

INDEX

Note: *Italicized* page references indicate photographs.

Almond
    Ciabatta French Toast, 90, 91
    -Cranberry Granola, 102
    and Pear Tartlets, Hand-Formed, 120, *121*
Apple
    Caramelized, Crêpes, 84, *85*
    Cinnamon-, Baked French Toast, *92*, 93
    -Raisin Turnovers, Spiced, 117
Apricot Chicken Salad, *168*, 169
Apricot Ginger Jam, 194
Asparagus with Poached Eggs and Parmesan, *74*, 75-76

Bacon
    and Egg Salad Sandwiches, 70
    -Scallion Scones, 108
    Waffles, Kathy's, 87
Banana-Raspberry Smoothie, 26
Bananas Foster, 183
Basil Pesto, 139
Beet and Artichoke Salad, 171-72, *173*
Berry(ies). *See also specific types*
    Three-, Compote, 189
Blackberry Bread Pudding, 96
Blueberry-Pineapple Smoothie, 27
Bread Pudding
    Blackberry, 96
    Strata 101; variations, 44-46, *45*
Burritos, Breakfast, 61
Butter, Honey, Hot or Cold, 195
Butters, Fruit, 196, *197*

Champagne and Cranberry with Mint, 33
Champagne Pimm's Cup, 34, *35*

Cheese
    Breakfast Burritos, 61
    Cheesy Cheddar Grits, 159
    Corn and Parmesan Fritters, 153
    Cream, Flavored, 198
    Goat, and Chive Hash Browns, *156*, 157
    Goat, and Roasted Tomatoes, Crunchy Zucchini Rounds with, 134, *135*
    Goat, Cake with Slow-Cooked Quince, 97-99, *98*
    Gooey Camembert in a Box with Cranberry-Black Pepper Compote, 154, *155*
    Gougères, 126-27
    Grilled Parmesan and Black Pepper Polenta, 160
    Mozzarella and White Nectarine Skewers with Pesto, 137-39, *138*
    Panini Finger Sandwiches; variations, 132-33
    Spinach and Cheddar Soufflé, 73
    and Tomato Galette, 146-48, *147*
Chicken
    Potstickers with Soy Dipping Sauce, 141-43
    Salad, Apricot, *168*, 169
Chickpea, Celery, and Tuna Salad, 176
Chocolate
    Chip Crumb Cake Muffins, 113-14, *115*
    -Hazelnut Spread, 190, *191*
    Hot Cocoa with Brown Sugar, 22
    melting, 192
    Waffles, *88*, 89
    White, Hot, with Mint, 24
    White, Hot, with Orange, 24, *25*
Cinnamon-Coffee Ice Cubes, 18

Cinnamon Sugar Doughnuts, 122
Coffee
    -Cinnamon Ice Cubes, 18
    Frozen Latte, 21
    Iced, Thai, 19
    Iced, with Cinnamon-Coffee Ice Cubes, 16, *17*
    preparing, 18
Coffee Cake, Quick Pear Streusel, *110*, 111
Corn and Parmesan Fritters, 153
Cornmeal. *See also* Polenta
    Ham and Vegetable Scrapple, 161
Cranberry
    -Almond Granola, 102
    Angel-Food Muffins, 116
    -Black Pepper Compote, Gooey Camembert in a Box with, 154, *155*
    and Champagne with Mint, 33
    Crêpes, Caramelized-Apple, 84, *85*
    Crêpes 101; variations, 55-56, *57*
    Crullers, Glazed, 123
    Cucumber, Yogurt, Poached Salmon with, 150-52, *151*
    Cucurumao, 62, *63*

Date-Orange Muffins, Moist, 112
Doughnuts, Cinnamon Sugar, 122
Drinks. *See also* Coffee
    Banana-Raspberry Smoothie, 26
    Chai Tea, 20
    Champagne and Cranberry with Mint, 33
    Champagne Pimm's Cup, 34, *35*
    Gale's 3-Alarm Bloody Mary, *36*, 37

Hot Cocoa with Brown Sugar, 22
Infused Lemonade, 30
Orange-Lime Juice with Grenadine, 31
Pineapple-Blueberry Smoothie, 27
Raspberry Lemonade, 28, 29
Tangerine-Pink Grapefruit Juice, 32
tea, preparing, 18
White Hot Chocolate with Mint, 24
White Hot Chocolate with Orange, 24, 25

Egg(s)
    and Bacon Salad Sandwiches, 70
    Baked, in Ham Cups, 68, 69
    Breakfast Burritos, 61
    Coddled, 77
    Cucurumao, 62, 63
    Fried Matzoh, 72
    Frittata 101; variations, 48–50, 49
    hard-boiled, preparing, 71
    Omelet 101; variations, 40, 41–43
    Poached, and Parmesan, Asparagus with, 74, 75–76
    Quail, Fried, on Eggnog French Toast, 140
    Quiche 101; variations, 51–54, 52
    Scrambled, and Salami, 60
    Spinach and Cheddar Soufflé, 73
    Strata 101; variations, 44–46, 45
    Torta Rustica, 65–67, 66
    Voodoo, in Toast, 64
Equipment, 202–3

Farro with Tomatoes and Parsley, 166, 167
French Toast
    Almond Ciabatta, 90, 91
    Baked Cinnamon-Apple, 92, 93

Eggnog, Fried Quail Eggs on, 140
    Panettone, 94
Frittata 101; variations, 48–50, 49
Fritters, Corn and Parmesan, 153
Fruit. See also specific fruits
    Butters, 196, 197
    Fresh, Salad, 188

Galette, Cheese and Tomato, 146–48, 147
Garlic, roasted, preparing, 47
Ginger Scones with Peaches and Cream, 106, 107
Gougères, 126–27
Granola, Cranberry-Almond, 102
Granola-Peach Parfait, 103
Grapefruit, Pink, -Tangerine Juice, 32
Grits, Cheesy Cheddar, 159

Ham
    Breakfast Burritos, 61
    Cups, Baked Eggs in, 68, 69
    Torta Rustica, 65–67, 66
    and Vegetable Scrapple, 161
Hazelnut-Chocolate Spread, 190, 191
Hazelnuts, peeling, 192
Honey Butter, Hot or Cold, 195
Horseradish Mustard, Spicy, 199

Ice Cubes, Cinnamon-Coffee, 18
Ingredients, 204

Lemonade, Infused, 30
Lemonade, Raspberry, 28, 29
Lemon Cream, 182
Lemon-Herb Vinaigrette, 165
Lime-Orange Juice with Grenadine, 31

Marshmallows, Homemade, 23
Matzoh, Fried, 72
Menus, 200–201

Muffins
    Chocolate Chip Crumb Cake, 113–14, 115
    Cranberry Angel-Food, 116
    Orange-Date, Moist, 112
Mustard, Spicy Horseradish, 199

Nectarine, White, and Mozzarella Skewers with Pesto, 137–39, 138
Noodle Kugel, Pineapple, 95
Nuts. See also Almond
    Chocolate-Hazelnut Spread, 190, 191
    hazelnuts, peeling, 192
    Sugared Walnuts, 101

Oats
    Cranberry-Almond Granola, 102
    Steel-Cut, with Sugared Walnuts, 100
Omelet 101; variations, 40, 41–43
Onion, Caramelized, Tarts, 149
Orange-Date Muffins, Moist, 112
Orange-Lime Juice with Grenadine, 31

Pancakes
    Buttermilk; variations, 80–82, 81
    Caramelized-Apple Crêpes, 84, 85
    Crêpes 101; variations, 55–56, 57
    Potato, Mini, with Smoked Salmon, 131
    Tender, 83
Panini Finger Sandwiches; variations, 132–33
Peaches and Cream, Ginger Scones with, 106, 107
Peach-Granola Parfait, 103
Peanut Butter and Jelly Turnovers, 118, 119
Pear(s)
    and Almond Tartlets, Hand-Formed, 120, 121
    and Rhubarb, Roasted, with Orange, 186

Pear(s) (*continued*)
    Streusel Coffee Cake, Quick,
        110, 111
    Waldorf Salad, 170
Pesto, 139
Pimm's Cup, Champagne, 34,
        35
Pineapple-Blueberry Smoothie,
        27
Pineapple Noodle Kugel, 95
Polenta, Parmesan and Black
        Pepper, Grilled, 160
Popovers, Herbed Mini, 128-30,
        129
Pork. *See also* Bacon; Ham;
        Sausage(s)
    Potstickers with Soy Dipping
        Sauce, 141-43
Potato(es)
    Goat Cheese and Chive Hash
        Browns, *156,* 157
    Pancakes, Mini, with Smoked
        Salmon, 131
    Salad, Vinaigrette, 174
Potstickers with Soy Dipping
        Sauce, 141-43
Pretzels, Soft Giant, 109

Quiche 101; variations, 51-54,
        52
Quince, Slow-Cooked, Goat
        Cheese Cake with, 97-99,
        98

Raspberry-Banana Smoothie,
        26
Raspberry Lemonade, *28,* 29
Rhubarb and Pears, Roasted,
        with Orange, 186

Salad dressings
    Dill Vinaigrette, 175
    Lemon-Herb Vinaigrette, 165
Salads
    Apricot Chicken, *168,* 169
    Beet and Artichoke, 171-72,
        173
    Chickpea, Celery, and Tuna,
        176
    Farro with Tomatoes and
        Parsley, 166, *167*

Fresh Fruit, 188
Pear Waldorf, 170
Vinaigrette Potato, 174
Wheat Berry, 164
Salami and Scrambled Eggs, 60
Salmon
    Poached, with Cucumber
        Yogurt, 150-52, *151*
    Smoked, Mini Potato
        Pancakes with, 131
Sandwiches, Bacon and Egg
        Salad, 70
Sandwiches, Panini Finger;
        variations, 132-33
Sausage(s)
    Fried Quail Eggs on Eggnog
        French Toast, 140
    Pork and Maple, Homemade,
        Patties, 158
    Salami and Scrambled Eggs,
        60
Scallion-Bacon Scones, 108
Scones,
    Bacon-Scallion, 108
    Ginger, with Peaches and
        Cream, 106, *107*
Scrapple, Ham and Vegetable, 161
Seafood. *See* Salmon; Tuna
Smoothie, Banana-Raspberry,
        26
Smoothie, Pineapple-Blue-
        berry, 27
Soufflé, Spinach and Cheddar,
        73
Soups
    Heirloom Tomato Bisque, 177
    Watermelon Gazpacho, *178,*
        179
Spinach
    and Cheddar Soufflé, 73
    Torta Rustica, 65-67, *66*
Spreads
    Apricot Ginger Jam, 194
    Chocolate-Hazelnut, 190, *191*
    Flavored Cream Cheeses, 198
    Fruit Butters, 196, *197*
    Hot or Cold Honey Butter, 195
    Nana's Strawberry Pre-
        serves, 193
    Spicy Horseradish Mustard,
        199

Strata 101; variations, 44-46,
        45
Strawberry(ies)
    Preserves, Nana's, 193
    roll-cutting, 185
    in Syrup, *184,* 185

Tangerine-Pink Grapefruit
        Juice, 32
Tartlets, Hand-Formed Pear
        and Almond, 120, *121*
Tarts, Caramelized Onion, 149
Tea, Chai, 20
Tea, preparing, 18
Tomato(es)
    and Cheese Galette, 146-48,
        147
    Cucurumao, 62, *63*
    Gale's 3-Alarm Bloody Mary,
        36, 37
    Heirloom, Bisque, 177
    Oven-Roasted, 136
    and Parsley, Farro with, 166,
        167
    Roasted, and Goat Cheese,
        Crunchy Zucchini Rounds
        with, 134, *135*
Torta Rustica, 65-67, *66*
Tuna
    Chickpea, and Celery Salad,
        176
    Wheat Berry Salad, 164
Turnovers, Peanut Butter and
        Jelly, *118,* 119
Turnovers, Spiced Apple-Raisin,
        117

Waffles, Bacon, Kathy's, 87
Waffles, Basic; variations, 86
Waffles, Chocolate, *88,* 89
Walnuts, Sugared, 101
Watermelon Gazpacho, *178,*
        179
Wheat Berry Salad, 164

Yogurt, Cucumber, Poached
        Salmon with, 150-52, *151*

Zucchini Rounds, Crunchy, with
        Roasted Tomatoes and
        Goat Cheese, 134, *135*